CW00419505

Racing the Wind

A Cumbrian Childhood

For my Mother

Racing the Wind

A Cumbrian Childhood

Patricia Nolan

MERLIN UNWIN BOOKS

First published in Great Britain by
Merlin Unwin Books, 2019

Merlin Unwin Books Ltd
Palmers House
Corve Street
Ludlow
Shropshire SY8 1DB
UK

www.merlinunwin.co.uk

ISBN 978-1-910723-97-5

Typeset in 13 point Bembo by Merlin Unwin Books
Printed by Jellyfish Solutions, UK

Contents

CHAPTER ONE

Dark Days, Silver Threads

N THE day I heard the news, I left my lunch untouched on the plate and wandered back down the dusty road to school, framed by the fell which lay under a lazy autumn haze. From the playground the sound of the girls playing a skipping game floated over the wall of the tiny playground. 'Salt, mustard, vinegar, pepper,' they chanted, squealing if someone was careless enough to catch a foot in the rope.

I went inside and sat at my desk. Our teacher asked us to write a story about being granted three wishes; I wrote one word, 'If...' but pressed down so hard that the lead in my pencil snapped. I did not sharpen it, but sat staring at the blue lines and red margins of my English book. Two girls asked if they could read out what they had written, but their words meant as little to me as the drone of bees over moorland heather, and I laid down an arm to cover the blank page in front of me. Some of the infants at the other end of the room listened, while others hummed and murmured to themselves in their own private language and drew mysterious shapes on their small slates.

At afternoon break we ran across the road to the stile, up some steps, through a small gap in the stone wall and into to a rocky field we called The Howe. I joined in a game of tag but wandered off after a few minutes to find my friend who was lying on her back counting the stream of small fluffy clouds overhead. I shook her arm.

'Barbara, listen, if I tell you something will you promise to keep it a secret?'

'Sixteen, seventeen…' She stopped counting and turned to look at me, her eyes wide, a trail of summer freckles sprinkled over her nose and the blue ribbon of one of her bunches trailing on the grass.

'Is it important?'

I nodded.

'Aw right. I promise.'

She looked serious enough to be entrusted with my secret so I bent to whisper in her ear.

She must have kept her word as school went on as usual until, on the Thursday, our teacher made herself a cup of tea at morning break and picked up *The Whitehaven News*.

'Good heavens!' she spluttered, looking at me

over the top of the newspaper. 'But, Pat, why didn't you tell me your father had died?'

Her mouth fell open and she stared at me without speaking. With a collective gasp the children followed suit, though many had heard by now.

'Blinkin' 'eck!!' one of the boys said. A silence followed.

'Who knew about this?'

A few people sheepishly raised a hand.

'Well,' she puffed, and then added, 'Oh dear!' It was as though my blood was turning to ice. I felt a great ache in my chest, and, laying my arms on the desk wept days of suppressed tears onto my reading book.

It was just not fair. For a start I did not live on a farm, help with the milking, look t'yows (check the ewes), pick taties or any other mysterious occupations. I was the only person in the school whose father voted Labour and now this had happened. I do not remember how the day evolved, only that I was treated carefully, which I hated.

Tragedies do not always happen without warning; sometimes they creep up with long shadows, deepening by the week, by the month, until one day the sun never comes out. My father had suffered from ill-health for as long as I could remember, sitting by the fire after his supper, eyes closed, in obvious pain from his duodenal ulcer, which today could no doubt be zapped by a

9

course of antibiotics. He had to make do with milky drinks and cream crackers. I had to be quiet after he had eaten his supper, which he digested with closed eyes and hands resting on his stomach.

One day in mid-September I returned home from school and burst through the front door to find two neighbours sitting in our best chairs, sipping tea.

'Where's Mum?'

'Upstairs with your dad. He's not so well.'

At that point my mother called me up.

Nervously I entered the bedroom. There was a fire flickering in the small grate by the bed, a sure sign someone was poorly. A strong smell of Dettol pervaded the room, a frightening, serious sort of smell. My father was lying propped up by two pillows; he looked pale and thin in his blue striped pyjamas, but he was smiling.

'Come over here.' He took hold of my hand.

'Now, I want you to be a good girl for Mummy. Do you promise?'

'Yes,' I whispered.

He squeezed my hand.

'And you must say your prayers every night.' He was a devout Catholic.

I did not reply, sensing finality in his words, and stepped back from the bed.

'Say goodbye to Daddy,' Mum said, gently propelling me forward, and he held out his arms to hug and kiss me, his skin cool and dry against my burning cheek. Bursting into tears I buried my face into the gold and black satin eiderdown, then was taken downstairs.

'Joe's had a haemorrhage,' said one of the tea drinkers in a low voice, as another neighbour arrived. Whatever that was, it must be something serious. Auntie Doris was a good friend and had been given the task of looking after me while my mother accompanied my father to the infirmary in Carlisle, sixty miles away. An ambulance must have arrived, but I never saw it; clutching my stuffed toy and a few books I went off to her cottage at the end of the row, where I was to spend the next three weeks.

At first I was miserable and terrified at the thought of bad news. No one around had a telephone but there was one at the local grocer's shop, where they kindly delivered messages if urgent. Then gradually I moved to a state of faint optimism; my father had been ill before and recovered. Why not this time? And so the days passed; soft early autumn days of hazy blue mornings and evening skies echoing with the sound of roosting crows in the nearby wood. I looked forward to my parents returning and picking up the thread of our lives again.

That is, till lunchtime on the 26th September. I left school as usual at midday and half ran, half skipped back to Auntie Doris's for something to eat. I was hungry and thought of the slice of luncheon meat with salad and a piece of bread and butter in store, not to

11

mention the spoonful of condensed milk I could pinch while she was in the pantry.

'Hello dear,' she said. 'I'll get your dinner.' But I noticed that her voice was flat and subdued. She sat down beside me.

'I got some news this morning,' she said. 'About your father.' She paused and took my hand. 'He's gone to heaven, to be with Jesus.'

She was looking out of the window as she spoke, towards the sky, so I looked too, for a split second wondering if she had caught a glimpse of him, but knew immediately that was silly; heaven was invisible. She hugged me and then we cried a little, and she explained that it was good he was in no more pain, and that my mother would be returning soon. Only two months ago my father and I had celebrated our birthdays together, he his fortieth and I my eighth.

A few days later I stood on the steps of our cottage watching my mother walk slowly up the lane towards me carrying her suitcase. As she drew near she stopped and stretched out her arms, and with the accumulated longing and misery of those weeks without her, I ran down the steps and hurtled into her arms; nothing could ever be as bad again, now that she was home.

But later that evening the neighbours came round to pay their respects clutching cake and home-made biscuits while my mother brewed some tea. At first the atmosphere was subdued, but gradually people began to chat, firstly about what had happened and then relaxed into more general talk. I refused to join them even after my mother called me over.

'I'm tidying my drawer,' I said, straightening the boxes of games again for the third time. I glowered at my dolls and threw the yoyo into a corner with a pile of puzzles. It was chilly away from the fire but I refused to budge.

Finally, after everyone had left, Mum put her arms around me and said, 'Now, tell me what's wrong?'

'You don't care that Daddy died!' my cheeks were burning. 'You were smiling and talking like you didn't care!' And I sobbed for a long time while she stroked my back and cuddled me.

At last she said, 'Now look, darling, of course I care, and we're both going to miss him a lot. But we have to act normally, even if we don't feel like it. Daddy wouldn't like us to cry all the time, now would he?'

'No,' I snuffled, though I wasn't sure.

And so began the long process of digging deep and burying my grief. The funeral was held at a Catholic church in his home town, but I did not go. It was thought it would upset me further, and that a funeral was no place for a child.

The following months were hard, both of us coping with our loss. I constantly scrutinised my mother's face for signs of suffering but she seemed to be behaving quite normally. Then one day I rushed home from school to be in time for *Mrs Dale's Diary* on the wireless at 3.45pm.

'Hello Mum!' I called, and then I saw her, sitting at the sewing machine by the window stitching a tartan skirt for me, catching the last of the November light. I noticed her face and stopped in my tracks; her eyes were red and puffy and I could see teardrops on her cheek. The idea that my mother should cry was appalling to me.

'Oh,' I said.

'Hello darling.' She went to make us a drink, but I could not speak. Then, as usual, I went to find a book and took myself off to a land of make-believe where there was always a happy ending.

The weather was drizzly and bleak during those months before Christmas, with little daylight as the days shortened. One afternoon I discovered a copy of *Little Women*, put aside for when I was older. Pleased to find something I had not read, I began, and, skipping a few words here and there, managed to follow the chronicle of the March family. When I reached Chapter 18, where Beth becomes ill and death seems to be a distinct possibility, I noticed the chapter was entitled 'Dark Days', and I thought: that's us, we are living through dark days.

And not only was my mother grieving, she was desperately worried about our finances; my father had left nothing due to bouts of illness, and the small legacy from my grandmother was drying up. There was no work in the valley out of the tourist season, which then was more low-key, and we had to live off a very meagre widow's pension, much of which disappeared in rent.

The worst days were Sundays, when my mother refused to leave her bed till midday.

'No,' she would say, 'get dressed and go and play,' and she would close her eyes and bury her face in the pillow.

But it was too cold without the fire lit, so I searched the house for reading matter, anything bearing print was acceptable, and like a squirrel, I took my hoard back to bed. Having read my books several times, I found old magazines of my mother's, and puzzled over short stories and serials of a romantic nature.

'*Stewart laid a steady hand on her shoulder. 'I'll always be here for you Melanie, you know that,' he said softly...*'

I perused *Woman's Weekly* from cover to cover, read the feeble Children's section with Dr. Owl's anecdote of the week, (Der Owl, I called him), inspected the knitting patterns for the boy and girl dolls, who must have had more outfits than Hollywood stars. Then finally, Mum would heave herself out of bed and our Sunday would begin.

But after Christmas, each day was blessed with a few extra rays of light – a cock-stride a day, the old folks said – and so it was with our lives. My mother, naturally resourceful, sent off to *Exchange and Mart* for leather skivers and a tool-kit, teaching herself to make purses, handbags, belts and children's slippers edged with rabbit fur, which were sold to relations and people in the valley. She helped two aged aunts and an uncle to spring-clean, pick fruit in their orchard, collect vegetables and bake bread; they enjoyed her lively company and were generous with us. I would arrive home from school to find a note on the table:

Dear Patsy. Gone to Esk Bank. Follow on your bike. Love Mum.

And we would return laden with vegetables, tomatoes, soft fruit, and in this first spring, cheerful bunches of daffs and forsythia, and a dripping, golden honey-comb. And at the approach of summer, the small café opened at the miniature railway station, offering employment for my mother through the season. Not full-time, but enough.

And then, an offer came, which I noticed with alarm that my mother was seriously considering. Our family doctor, still upset he had failed to notice my father was dying of lung cancer, mentioned that his parents were looking for someone to keep house for them; it was a large place with plenty of room for us all. And it was in a town called Newcastle-under-Lyme.

'It sounds a horrid place,' I said, with the benefit of absolutely no knowledge at all.

But the offer hung over our heads like a swarm of bees, dangerous and threatening.

One evening I leant out of my bedroom window, and looked over to the mountains opposite, the heather turning them purple in the sunset. My mother was below dead-heading the flowers and I caught the scent of our deep pink, old-fashioned rose.

'Mum,' I called, 'we'll never leave here, will we?'

She smiled up at me. 'No darling,' she said, 'we won't.'

And she kept her word.

In under a year's time our lives would change irrevocably, but that summer our recovery was underway. Relations came to visit; we went for long walks past hay fields shimmering with cow parsley and marguerites, down lanes crammed with dog-roses, honeysuckle and willow herb. And I returned to extreme acts of daring with my cronies, hollering from tree-tops, dangling off branches, leaping into green rock-pools, and best of all, flying down the fell, arms outstretched, racing the wind.

CHAPTER TWO

Guided by the Moon

PALE light had crept into the room, making me think morning had arrived at last. Keeping an eye on my mother who was snoring gently into her pillow, I slipped out of bed and tiptoed over the icy lino to the window and pulled back the curtain. On the inside of every pane were patterns of stars magically etched.

When I breathed on a small patch of glass and rubbed it, I saw a world with all colour removed; snowy fell tops, black rocks and crags with a white sprinkling, grey fields, and below me, our garden of dormant plants and frosty tussocks of grass. The earth was frozen, with no movement of birds, animals or people, as if time had stopped.

It was clearly still very early on this, the last day of 1950.

I shivered, crept back into bed and snuggled up to my mother's back, but was unable to sleep, my whole head being covered in white knots. The previous night my hair had been washed, my long, very straight locks divided into sections and wound round strips of cloth, which were then tied firmly to resist any nocturnal turbulence.

Later that morning, the rags would be carefully removed to reveal, miraculously, a headful of corkscrew ringlets, a glamorous replacement of my usual plaits. It was all in aid of the annual Fancy Dress Party in the school, starting at two o' clock; and today, for the first time since my father died in September, I felt a small bubble of excitement which refused to budge, even when a heavy cloud seemed to have settled permanently over our house.

After lunch we packed up our contribution to the tea, and carefully folded my costume. I was to be The Lavender Lady. My dress had been dyed and cut down from an old bridesmaid's gown; it was gathered at the waist, falling into a full skirt, with tiny covered buttons right down the back. I loved the abundant silkiness brushing against my legs, the bonnet that tied under my chin, and the basket of dried lavender hanging over my arm. How could I fail to win?

The cloakroom at school was crammed with small bodies wriggling into costumes and mothers tugging them into shape. My ringlets were holding out, arranged to peep out of the bonnet at each side, the buttons were hurriedly fastened, and the basket… the basket? Ah, there, in the corner, with some shoes and a pair of somebody's knickers stuffed in. Then it was off into the schoolroom for the grand parade. There must have been around twenty-five costumes, though it felt like more, with the usual clowns, tramps, Robin Hoods, Winston Churchills and other popular characters of the day. My favourite was the Policeman and the Cook, worn by our neighbour, and which, like all successful outfits, appeared every year. It was ingeniously assembled, half a helmet, half chef's floppy hat, eye-glass, truncheon, wooden spoon, trouser leg and apron, with a neat dividing line down his middle.

He won his class, which was for Originality. As usual. I was in the Neat category, and paraded my wares around the room with high hopes.

'First prize... Snow-white!' called our M.C., an elderly gentleman who had had a good war, the Great War, that is.

Snow-white simpered up for her prize with eleven looks of pure hatred in her trail, and waved a large and rather ugly doll in a box.

'Second prize...The Lavender Lady!'

I received two bars of chocolate, and felt the winner. In those days of post-war rationing, a chocolate bar was always carefully divided, a couple of squares each, with the remains hidden away for tomorrow.

There was little money in this remote valley but we were mostly well-fed; in farming communities there was always a good supply of milk, butter and vegetables. Before my father died we had kept a pig in

21

a sty on the fell, my mother's sausage being a winner. And everyone had hens, foxes permitting.

Now it was time for games, when we exchanged our exotic costumes for day wear, in my case, a kilt and natural wool Shetland jumper with a band of heathery fair-isle across my chest, knitted by my mother. The ringlets were fading fast so were briskly brushed out, leaving a waterfall of waves which I refused to have tied back.

There were two villages in the valley, ours, higher into the mountains, being by far the smaller, but today inhabitants of both were crowded into our little, one-room school. Our games were more of a physical nature.

Nuts in May! someone shouted. The boys pressed their backs against the wall and said it was too sissy, but were prised away and shoved into line.

'*Here we go gathering nuts in May, nuts in May, nuts in May*', we sang in a variety of keys, skipping forwards and backwards.

'*Here we go gathering nuts in May, on a cold and frosty morning.*'

'*Who shall we have for nuts in May...?*' Pick a girl, to much delighted screaming.

'*And who shall we have to take her away...?*' Pick a boy. Deafening squeals, followed by desperate tug o' war between the two, then begin again. There followed some wild chasing games like *The Farmer's in his Den* resulting in a couple of grazed knees, and finally we reached fever pitch with the game of 'Postman's Knock'.

'Two letters and a parcel for number seven!' someone would shout with great bravado, but once in the cloakroom away from the crowd, the delivery was no more than a quick, bashful peck on the cheek.

After that, anarchy prevailed: boys skidded up and down in their lace-up boots, girls held hands and twizzled dizzily, and I did a handstand against the wall and tore someone's painting of Scafell with my heel. A father from higher up the room had had enough. He stood up. He did *not* say, 'OK guys, now listen up.' What he said was, 'Shurrup you kids, *now*, or you'll git no tea!'

At the mention of tea, like a fire doused by water, we calmed down, and when desks had been arranged in rows, we sat and gazed expectantly at the mothers, who, homely in their flowered pinnies, brought in an enormous tea-urn and laid out the party fare, every scrap made by them. There was much intense whispering amongst them over the provenance of the different items.

'Who made this cake, Betty? Ah, thought so.'

'Are these your mince-pies, Mary?' I heard someone say.

'Yes.'

'Smashin'. Lovely and crisp,' was the indistinct reply.

I turned to see my mother smile. The day was improving by the minute.

I avoided the trifle, jelly and cream, even though they were sprinkled with hundreds and thousands. After the first spoonful from the bowl, an unattractive pinkish sauce had gathered in the bottom, so I stuck to sausage-rolls, chocolate log and fairy cakes. When finally our stomachs were as tight as drums and the mothers had finished supping tea, all was cleared away for the next event, my favourite: The Social.

This involved members of the audience standing up and 'doing a turn', which could be a poem, a few jokes, a funny story or a song, accompanied by our teacher if they so wished. I had learnt a poem by R.L. Stevenson by heart, but, like the spy with his cyanide tablet, it was likely to remain under wraps. There were certain perennials, like our first song for instance, which was all about tea. We enjoyed the familiarity, and joined the farmer's wife in the last line of each verse, singing lustily, *'For a cup o' mi camomile tea'*.

What we enjoyed particularly was when something went wrong, and we were not disappointed. A girl, senior to me by a few years, started off quite sweetly with, *There's a Hole in my Bucket*, then suddenly burst into tears and dashed out of the room, so we never heard how the hole was to be mended. Such excitement! Then we had a rendition of *There's a one-eyed yellow idol to the north of Kathmandu* by someone with an eye-patch and a posh voice, and the usual *Albert and the Lion* which made us laugh. The highlight is often the unexpected, and this year was no exception.

A young father stood up, his fair skin flushing pink, hands behind his back, and sang a hunting song. His eyes were fixed on the window, and I wondered if he was seeing the fox streaking up the fell with the hounds giving chase, weaving their way through the woods, tongues hanging out. He had a high tenor voice, true and as smooth as the cream on the trifle. A hush fell over the room, and a crying baby stopped in his tracks and turned his round grey eyes on to the singer. There was also a joining in bit, which pleased us,

'Tally ho! And here's to good health, tally ho!' we all warbled, and clapped rapturously as, with head ducked, he returned to his seat.

During the entertainment I scanned the room to find my mother; she was standing with her arms folded, leaning against a wall by the window which was open a few inches. Her dark curly hair blew back from her face, pink from all the tea-brewing. She was not watching the performers but seemed to be thinking about something quite different.

By now, the sun had dipped below the horizon and the light was fading rapidly. Parents and many of the children drifted off, but other adults were arriving for the Whist Drive, a serious business which required children, if they stayed, to be completely silent. Desks were pushed into groups of four, and people took to their seats. It seemed odd to me that my desk, which I had identified by the circle of blots round the inkwell, where I spent much of my time poring over Maths problems, should have the vicar eating his trifle off it, and now someone playing cards on its lid.

'Spades trumps!' the M.C. called and cards were shuffled and expertly dealt.

'What's trumps?' asked an elderly farmer.

'Spades, Tom!' somebody yelled in his ear, then a concentrated hush descended, and a cosy fug of cigarette smoke collected over their heads. There was a coal fire at each end of the room, and we children half-dozed around the iron fire-guards, our cheeks growing red, and watched the reflection of the flames catch the brass oil-lamps hanging from the ceiling.

Bored, I wandered to the window and peered out. I could see the outline of the hills opposite, and a group of black trees to the right, waving slightly. A ghost of a moon was rising behind them, and I wondered if Daddy was looking down at us, at Mum playing cards and me being bored; you could probably see everything from heaven.

After what seemed like a lifetime of cards being thumped down, of puffing and sighing and coughing, the games finally ended, and desks were pushed to the edge of the room for the final fling which would take us to midnight. We were starting to wilt, but, when the M.C. shouted, 'Take your partners please for the *Paul Jones*!' we were all on the floor joining hands, as our teacher bustled down the room to take her seat at the piano. We jigged round the room, anticipating who we would be opposite when the music stopped. I enjoyed the tune of *The Palais Glide*, waited hopefully to be put into sets for *The Dashing White Sergeant*, joined in *The Hokey Cokey* with vigour, and stamped our hardest in the *St. Bernard's Waltz*; the quick-steps and foxtrots were left for the adults.

The miracle happened during *The Dashing White Sergeant*. Before I was gathered up to join in, I saw two hefty ladies stamping down the room arm-in-arm with a thinner person in the middle; that person in the green dress was my mother, and what's more she was laughing, not polite laughing, but as if she could not stop, even if she had wanted to. I watched them gallop, swing and tap out the steps up and down the room, raising small puffs of dust from between the floorboards.

For the first time for ages my mother was happy, and I was glad for her; finally I realised we were allowed to enjoy ourselves.

As midnight approached, men began to arrive, glazed eyes, loose mouths, unsteady of gait. Disapproving glances and comments came from the women. 'How much have *you* had?' But we children were partial to witnessing a bit of intoxication, and if the men fell over, so much the better.

Shortly before twelve our crackly school radio was switched on. Then came the chimes of Big Ben, all the way from London. At the last 'boing' we joined hands in a big circle for *Auld Lang Syne*, and the M.C. shouted, 'Happy New Year everybody!'

27

'Happy New Year!' we yelled back, and everybody kissed everybody else in the room. Then, silence and up straight for the National Anthem.

Muffled in coat, scarf and mittens, clutching our bags, we finally left.

'Night Mary!'

'Happy New Year!'

'Mind how you go!'

'It's like daylight out here!'

My eyes felt heavy, as it was long past my bedtime. We set off up the road, switching off the flashlight; our way was guided by the moon, which was almost full.

'It was good, wasn't it Mum?'

'Did you enjoy it?' She squeezed my hand through her rabbit fur glove.

Through the white light we walked, hedgerows glittering, snowy fells sleeping; across the field we scrunched, past the river frozen at the edges, stiff reeds pointing skywards like silver swords, and down the path towards our cottage into a new and better year.

CHAPTER THREE

Village School

I T IS not unusual for pupils to absent themselves from school on occasions, but rare, as in my case, to abscond *to* school.

By the time I was four my parents had taught me to read, and from that time on I harboured a deep yearning to go to school, where there would be shelves of story books, games and a wealth of playmates.

One afternoon in May, when the sun streamed over the field opposite, and month-old lambs leaped over their mothers, tails bobbing like catkins in the wind, I disappeared down the lane in the direction of school.

I arrived, as I had hoped, at the moment the children were spilling out of the door over to the field opposite for afternoon break. My cousin, Valerie, who was two years my senior and had encouraged my escapade, saw me and ran up to take my hand.

'Come and play with us,' she said.

Some of the big girls, now fifteen and ready to leave in the summer, petted and tickled me and replaited one of my pigtails, knotting the red ribbon with tight efficiency. I joined in a game of tag and screamed with the rest when I was chased; but all too soon the bell, dangling high up on the end wall of the building, gave its sonorous clang, and people began to head for the stile and cross the road into school. I did not join them.

'Come with us.' Valerie tried to coax me in but I hung back. Then an older girl said, 'She won't mind. Honestly.' So timidly I followed them inside and sat with Valerie at her desk, our legs squashed up on the bench seat. A hush fell over the room and everyone was smiling.

'What?' said Miss Jackson, looking round. Then she spotted me and burst out laughing.

'What are *you* doing here?'

On a bad day I would have received a cuff round the ear and a flea inside it for good measure, but today her mood was mellow, and I mistakenly thought that's how it would always be.

'Oh, please can she stay, Miss Jackson, please?' Valerie begged.

'Well, all right. Just for this afternoon. But then you must wait till September when you are meant to start,' and then she began one of her history lessons about the Roman invasion, and how the soldiers marched past our school up to the fort perched high at the head of the valley and what weapons they would be carrying, at which point I saw a boy glance nervously out of the window. But I took the opportunity to look round this holy sanctum to which I had at last gained entry.

The building was Victorian, constructed of local granite of a pinkish hue, due to a seam of iron ore on the fell, and consisted of one long room with an open fire at each end, and a small cupboard where the PT equipment was kept. Through a low door down two steps lay a tiny cloakroom, and behind, luckily in a semi-open construction, were the toilets, from which, particularly in hot weather, there emanated a stench overlaid by the medicated whiff of Jeyes Fluid. The toilets themselves were like wooden boxes with a round hole cut out, which were called dry closets because there was no water supply laid on; they had to be emptied every Friday, where exactly we never knew. The teacher was given the luxury of her own private cubicle.

The walls of the room were of a creamy yellow colour, but were mostly taken up by windows, a long one at each end, and four divided into small panes down the road side of the room. Several noticeboards were pinned with paintings and pieces of writing, but it was the bluebells I remember, five jam jars of them placed along a shelf, together with some twigs which had burst out into small pale leaves; I could smell their green fragrance and still remember the snippets of sunlight on the glass jars. I also sniffed the complex blend of unwashed bodies, (daily showers being decades away), burning coal, dust from books, chalk and floorboards, and talcum powder from the teacher as she wafted by.

'Here's some paper.' A boy slung a piece in front of me so I shared Valerie's crayons and drew my usual house with four windows and lots of flowers in the garden, and said it was the Roman fort. At 3.30 I ran home highly excited to regale my mother with every detail of my hour at school.

'I thought that's where you must have gone,' she said, smiling. We were always assumed to be safe unless there was good reason to doubt it.

So early in September I set off, expectations high, with a new pencil and rubber in my pocket. The teacher arrived, puffing slightly, on her old bicycle, and ushered us unruly mob into school.

Miss Jackson was a stout, bespectacled woman in her middle years, with the sort of hips that could swing a kilt, and often did, paired with a Shetland wool jumper; her brown hair was plaited and pinned round her head. She was a woman of moods, and today's was unpredictable.

'New infants that end!' she shouted, and a handful of us shuffled to the small tables and chairs for which I was already too tall. We sat quietly while the others were arranged in the rows of desks in some sort of order. We stared while they pushed and shoved and the teacher shrieked; there was danger in the air, and at one point there was a cracking sound, of irate hand on bare thigh, followed by a series of wails. When calm at last prevailed we were given a black slate each with some chalks and were directed to copy from the board. By the end of the day we got to H is for Hat. I sat and smouldered.

'Well, *tell* her,' said my mother that evening, but it was not easy.

The next day we started with 'I is for Ink' and finally I laid down my chalk.

'Come on,' she called from her desk. 'Learn your letters and then you'll be able to read.'

My moment had come. 'But I *can* read,' I replied in a small voice.

'Oh no. Not yet. But if you work hard you will soon learn.' It was hopeless. Then my dear cousin spoke up from further down the room.

'She *can* Miss Jackson. She can read.'

Muttering things like 'impossible' and 'I don't think so', she marched to a book shelf and thrust Beacon Reader book 2 before me and said, 'There. Read that.'

And then, aged five, there followed the one moment of academic glory of my whole career.

'Once upon a time, there lived a beautiful princess...'

'Oh!' said Miss Jackson. 'Well, we'd better move

you,' and I was released from my uncomfortable habitat to take residence in a proper desk, and proudly I laid out my pencil and rubber on the ridge by the inkwell and stretched out my legs.

There must have been around twenty-five children in the room at that time, though a year later everyone over eleven was sent to the school lower down the valley, and when I left the numbers had fallen to sixteen. But with the wide age range it must have been difficult for one teacher to keep us all busy and educated. In english and maths we tended to have individual workbooks, and progressed at our own pace, and in the occasional geography and history lesson most people sat and listened. Every morning began with a bible story, important, as it was a church school. Inspectors arrived occasionally, and seemed to approve, particularly of our maths tens and units equipment, which consisted of reeds collected from the Howe, snipped into bundles of ten and knotted with wool, leaving single ones for units.

'Good use of the environment,' they remarked, not knowing we had spent the previous day putting the chaotic tins of reeds in order.

But, as was often the case at that time, we were ruled by fear. You could be puzzling out a problem involving carrots, rabbits and their daily consumption, when suddenly you would receive a hard box on the ears, and were told not to be so stupid and *think*, which of course had the opposite effect. Legs were slapped, often in temper, or the cane would appear for more serious 'misdemeanours'. Once when we naughtily ignored the bell at the end of playtime, the whole school lined up and were caned. My mother had been taught here by the same teacher, and her memories were similar. They were the bad days, when you scarcely dared to move in case you were punished.

But there were good times too. Because the road had little traffic, anything that passed aroused our interest, and if we heard the heavy clip-clop of hooves, someone would shout, 'Here comes Bill on his horse and cart!' and we would all down tools and run to knock on the window and shout, 'How do, Bill!' and he would raise his stick and call, 'Hello there!' And normally there would be no complaint. Then sometimes, on a sunny day, we were told that if we worked hard in the morning we would go on a nature walk later.

'Hurray!' we would shout, and lowered our heads in an effort to look studious.

Then we wandered down the lanes, frothy with blossom, were taught the names of trees and wild flowers, and picked large bunches to take back; the infants trailed behind and older girls took their hands and coaxed them along. We were instructed on what to do if we were bitten by an adder. It sounded fearsome.

'You must take a penknife and cut along the bite, then suck out the poison.'

'Ugh!' we all went.

'And,' she added, looking at me, 'your great uncle died at the age of four from a snake bite.' Unusual, but true.

The school was without water and electricity. At lunch time sandwiches of a disgusting nature were delivered by a van; they were of cheap ham and mustard, accompanied by a sad-looking green apple. We nibbled the crusts and ignored the fruit. Later, hot meals were delivered, only marginally tastier.

But on hard winter days, the teacher heated up a large urn of cocoa on the fire to warm us up, and sometimes, to our great amusement, when she had boiled a kettle for herself, like a magician she would remove an egg from it and place it in an egg-cup, and then brew herself a pot of tea. The water had to be collected in buckets each morning from the vicarage, which was a few minutes walk away and had an outside tap. Two trustworthy boys were accorded the job, and there was always keen competition for this short reprieve.

On dark afternoons in December and January, when our northern light was fading, the brass oil lamps hanging from the ceiling had to be lit, and whilst the glow was soft and sent flickering shadows up the wall, by 2.30 it was growing dim.

'Can you see what you're doing, children?' our teacher would ask us.

Knowing what was coming, we would wrinkle our noses.

'Not really.'

'Right. Books away then,' and whilst plasticine was distributed to the infants so they could make models and doze by their fire, we gathered round the other end of the room, jockeying for a warm position, and listened to stories of Ratty and Mole in the Wild Wood, or giggled over the antics of Brer Rabbit and friends. Always, someone would fall asleep, and gradually cheeks turned rosy, the room darker, and peace descended until home-time.

The highlight of the summer term was our trip to the seaside, an unremarkable village ten miles away with a wide sandy beach. We left on our local bus hired for the day, already investigating our packed lunches, and could not have been more excited had we been heading for Monte Carlo. We paddled, or swam if it was hot, while our teacher buried her head in *The Times* and sometimes dozed off.

My grandmother had also attended this school, a three mile walk over the moors every morning, and sometimes I would imagine her, and later my mother, playing on the Howe, sliding down The Spire, an enormous rock like an elephant's back, petticoats flying, clogs swinging, black hair blowing in the wind. There were many Norse place names in our area: *garth, thwaite, ghyll, tarn and fell; howe* meant hill. There was a flat area in the bottom, which rose up to a rocky slope with deciduous woodland behind, and this was where we played when the weather was fine.

One heady summer our teacher contracted shingles, and was absent for half a term. Three supply teachers tried their hand at taming us but left in despair after a few days. The last one disappeared after the first day, complaining we were a bunch of young hoodlums, so in desperation the vicar was obliged to teach us, unorthodox in his methods, but harmonious. There were dictations from *The Guardian*, ('not *quite* right but a good shot'), and mental arithmetic on the Howe, lying in the sun, occasionally giving an answer, 'sixty-four' or 'seventy-two', chewing grass, picking at moss and watching small woolly clouds float over the fell-tops.

With classmates from Boot Village School. The author is second from right

CHAPTER FOUR

Elderlies, Family and the Old Ways

LD people were valued then, for their memories of past times, for cosy kitchens, with dogs and cats sighing by an open fire, old wall-clocks with their loud ticks chiming the hour from front parlours, and for the potency of their elderberry wine. They sat puffing on pipes and supping tea, telling unlikely yarns from their youth, of days before the road was tarred and of hair-raising incidents on the mountain pass leading out of the valley. They chuckled, shifted arthritic joints on padded rocking chairs, pinched our cheeks and gave us half-a-crown. They had seen everything: celebrations, tragedies, coronations and two world wars. When they died, people gathered round the grave to the scent of trampled grass and the sound of the river, and someone would remark quietly, 'Ay, there's another old character gone,' and everyone would nod in agreement, thinking of all the questions that remained unasked.

There had been few changes in the way of life in the valley where my grandmother's family farmed for centuries, tracing directly back to the 1600s. Horses and carts trundled up and down the same pink dust roads, hay was raked and laden on horsecarts to barns, bracken cut and stored for bedding, grain harvested, crops gathered, cows milked, sheep sheared and ancient dry stone wall gaps repaired. At my local school our half term holiday at the end of October was always referred to as 'Tatie Pickin' Week', when all the children would lend a hand in gathering in the potatoes before the frost set in. It was in the 1950s that the Ferguson tractor first appeared, changing the life of a farmer for ever.

But in the Lakeland valleys sheep rule, and with us it was Herdwicks, noted for their hardiness and ability to withstand the bitter weather out on the fells; occasionally they have been discovered in snow drifts, keeping alive by nibbling their own wool. They are left to graze freely on the fell but learn to stay in their own 'heaf' or home territory, the ewes passing on the knowledge to their lambs. They usually spend winter out on the fells, checked occasionally by the farmer for any problems that might have arisen. On a fine day in spring, weather noted, lunch packed, liquid refreshment sorted, the farmer would set out for the fell to collect his flock: gathering, it was called.

I often seemed to be around on these days, when there was excitement in the air, dogs barking and the owner calling them to heel: 'e-Jess-e-Jess e-Jess' echoed down the street to the sound of sturdy boots on the tarmac. The farmer would call in the shop for chocolate or a can of drink, smart in his tweed jacket and clean shirt, holding a large walking stick with a carved handle. He would be accompanied by his son or any other willing helpers. My mother always inquired as to what time they would be returning.

'Nay now,' would be the amused reply.

But usually it was in the late afternoon when you heard the distant bleating of the herd descending the fell and my mother would run out with a stick to guard her flowers in the small garden by the road, trying, mostly in vain, to prevent the sheep from snatching at the tasty morsels on offer.

At her cries of 'Get off!' the farmer would hoot with laughter as he brandished his stick and shouted at the dogs. The noise made by the sheep was deafening, and even my mother had to admit it was a fine sight.

I was lucky that my mother took a keen interest in the past and told many stories about the old times, resisting any exaggeration or embellishment.

My grandmother, Hannah Hartley was born in 1894 on a remote farm over a steep fell, two and a half miles from the village, and from the age of five she walked to school, weather permitting. Sometimes a horse and cart might give her a lift back up the hill, otherwise her small legs toiled up the winding road over the fell each evening. In spite of her absences she left school at the age of twelve with beautiful copper-plate handwriting, and a sound knowledge of grammar and spelling. She was a favourite with the teacher, who kept up his spirits with regular slugs from a bottle of whisky in the drawer of his teacher's desk.

She married George Massicks at the age of eighteen, and, with great efficiency, produced six children, each two years apart, three boys and three girls. My mother, the second child, remembered the year 1918 when, at the age of four, she was sitting on a swing in the garden leaning back trying to fly over the tree-tops, when she saw a strange man in uniform walking up the hill towards her. He scooped her up in his arms and kissed her, the bristles of his moustache scratchy on her cheek

'Hello Mary,' he said. It was her father, who had joined up in 1914, back from the horrors of war of which he rarely spoke.

My grandfather's return ended the gentle way of life to which the family had grown accustomed. He was head gamekeeper on a large estate stretching from the coast to the moorlands above the valley. He reared partridges, grouse and pheasants, and during the season organised shoots, when a flock of gentlemen in Harris-tweed plus-fours bearing picnic hampers would arrive at their house, guns at the ready. After eating, they would leave the remnants for the children, who fell upon a selection of unfamiliar and exotic fare, including Fortnum's veal and ham pies, pâté, quails eggs, chicken in aspic and tiny crunchy biscuits. Beaters arrived, cocker and springer spaniels yelped and jumped around, impatient to be off, while the children watched from a safe distance, peeping through the bushes at the shenanigans of dogs and men.

The gamekeeper's cottage was in fact a large, five-bedroomed house on the edge of a wood, with an acre or two of land which my grandfather, a strong, resourceful man, put to good use. He grew every vegetable you could name, together with pear, apple, damson and plum trees, bushes bearing gooseberries, raspberries, blackcurrants, redcurrants, and, to the

Dalegarth Cottage where my gamekeeper grandfather lived

children's delight, he dug a large strawberry bed. Before the days of refrigerators, anything not immediately consumed had to be preserved: onions, cabbage and cauliflower were chopped and pickled, pears and plums bottled in large Kilner jars, and much of the fruit was made into jam. My grandmother baked all their bread and cakes, flour and oats being available at the local mill, which had been part of the valley since medieval times. The butcher's van visited once a week, and only a few necessities such as salt, sugar and candles did she purchase from the local grocer's. There was always a pig or two being fattened up, and also several goats, which became the bane of my grandmother's life.

'Those blasted goats!' the normally gentle lady would cry, as they escaped their tether yet again, infiltrated the kitchen and ate the bread dough she had set to rise by the fire, taking a snatch at the washing waving from the line on departing.

My grandfather was a strict disciplinarian, the children never being allowed to speak at mealtimes. Sometimes my mother would whisper to her mother, 'Is it goat's?' if there was milk on the table, something she detested.

'Don't be so fussy!' a voice would bark from the head of the table.

Occasionally my mother's little brother, crazy about animals, would dig her in the ribs and point, and she would look down to see the whiskery face of a ferret poking out of his pocket. Later, in his teens, Bill had his own dog, a beautiful golden Labrador, which he adored. One day it escaped into a field and began to chase the sheep, became over-excited, and sank its teeth into one of them. Once a dog had tasted blood it was judged they could never be trusted again, so he was told the dog must be destroyed. His father offered to perform this terrible task for him, but Bill refused.

'Lassie's mine,' he said, 'so it's my job to do it,' and he took his gun and led her off to the woods, where he dug a grave and laid her to rest. It took him months to recover from the trauma.

From the left: grandfather, mother and her five siblings

45

In spite of the size of their family, at the beginning of the Second World War they were allocated two evacuees from Newcastle, brothers of around 9 and 11 years old, pale, miserable, skinny little boys, constantly scratching. After a thorough scrubbing and delousing in a hot bath and one of my grandfather's special hair cuts, a razor over the scalp with a small flap of hair left at the front, they began to enquire as to the whereabouts of the picture-house and the fish and chip shop.

'Hmm. A good twenty mile walk,' was the reply.

But gradually they became used to this new way of life; accompanied by my grandfather on to the moors, they went out tracking foxes on frosty nights, swam in the tarns and rivers, played with the dogs and became rosy-cheeked country boys. They adored my grandmother, who fed and clothed them with the same love and care she had shown her own children. When the war ended and it was time for them to leave the valley, they were inconsolable at leaving this idyllic life for their drab worn-torn city; but every summer, well into adulthood, they returned to visit, having become fine young men who, on one visit to the valley, were devastated to hear that my grandmother had died suddenly of a stroke.

'She was so kind to us,' they said. 'She was our mother in those years. We'll never forget her.'

Two sons in the family were involved in the war, the third being exempt as he worked on the land. Bill, the youngest, deducting a year from his age, joined up towards the end, was taught to drive jeeps and trucks and was in no danger, but John, an intelligent, sensitive young man of twenty-one, found himself on the front line, causing great worry to his parents. At one point, his letters suddenly stopped; each morning they anxiously waited but no news, till at last, as weeks turned to months, his mother began to walk down the drive every morning to the road to meet the post which was delivered on foot. After weeks of trudging down the path between the enormous beech tree in a woodland of deciduous trees and the guttering river, one morning she saw Winnie, the post girl, running down the hill, smiling and waving a white envelope.

'Hannah, Hannah! A letter from John!'

With tears of relief she tore into the letter. 'Some silly b----- from our side threw a shell which landed right beside me, and I was in hospital for weeks,' he wrote. 'Now I'm on a rest-cure in Egypt,' and a photo of him standing with his arms behind his back looking tanned and healthy fell out of the envelope. She did no more work that day but sat reading the letter till she knew it by heart.

No more than a year later, John was returning home on leave for a week. He took the train from London to the small seaside station where he caught the local bus home. It was mid-winter and an icy wind blew in from the sea. Exhausted, he climbed on to the bus as night was drawing in, threw his knapsack on the rack and collapsed on to a seat.

'Pity about your father,' Jack remarked. He pronounced it like 'gather'. He switched on the engine. 'Oh?' said John. 'What about him?'

'Died last week.' And he changed into second, his favourite gear, and began to negotiate a hair-pin bend.

And so John learned of his father's sudden death at the age of fifty-seven from encephalitis lethargica, causes unknown. A strong, healthy man when he last saw him, John was stunned and he stared out of the window, at fells patchy with snow and trees skeletal in the January gloom, trying to absorb this piece of news so carelessly delivered.

I wish I had known my Nana. She was shy and tender-hearted, as it was described then, a trait which was passed down through the family, a modest, but able woman. Not only did she raise a family of six healthy children and two evacuees, take in bed and breakfast visitors as her children grew up, serve home-made teas on the lawn to tourists on the way to the waterfall, but she also regularly won a prize in writing competitions in *John Bull*, a popular magazine of the time, inventing slogans and short descriptions. My mother remembered this because each time she won, Nana cashed the postal order and bought toys for the children, hoops to bowl down the drive, a pogo stick, yoyos and various ball games.

I have only one single memory of my grandmother, arriving at our cottage one afternoon, slightly out of breath, wearing a long black coat, heeled lace-up shoes, dark hair drawn from her round face into a bun, and gold wire glasses. I remember my mother's voice, pleased and surprised, 'Hello mother!' as normally it was us who visited her, because she was quite a walk away. So we made her a cup of tea. I was four years old. Later that same year she died suddenly of a stroke at the age of fifty-two. My mother kept her round wire glasses in a drawer for many years.

Aunt Liza, Aunt Annie and Uncle Harry all lived together lower down the valley in a detached Victorian house with fell views and small rooms. They were actually my great-great aunts and uncle, and although only in their mid-seventies around the time of my father's death, they seemed very ancient to me. The sisters had been widowed with no children whilst their brother was a bachelor.

Although siblings, they could not have been more different. Aunt Annie was tall and thin, with a back as straight as her silver-topped cane. Her complexion was sallow and quite wrinkled, and she bore the expression of someone who was about receive a great injustice and generally took a pessimistic view of life. But she was extremely smart in her appearance, a real Edwardian lady with long strings of pearls, neat costumes, high heels and hats sporting a galaxy of hatpins. She had a cosmopolitan air about her, perhaps due to the fact she had lived in Colwyn Bay for many years, returning to the valley when her husband retired. On special occasions she wore her fox furs, muzzle, paws and tail intact, arousing considerable interest in the canine world which she handled with a few none too gentle taps of her cane.

The siblings squabbled constantly, though Aunt Liza was a much softer person, and of a mournful disposition, especially after her slight stroke, and sat swaying in her rocking chair lamenting her husband's death. She repeated all of her sentences twice.

'Poor Jack, I say poor Jack,' and tears would roll down her cheeks. This irritated Uncle Harry beyond measure.

'Stop thee moaning, woman! He was an auld feller and he had a good life.' And he would stomp off to see to his bees or collect the eggs.

Sometimes she would glance at me and remember that my father had died.

'Poor laal Pat, I say poor laal Pat,' which infuriated me.

'Oh, she's fine,' my mother would say, to deflect her pity. And then, perhaps to make up for my sad loss, she would take down her Beefeater tin from the mantelpiece, which contained Old Fashioned Mint Humbugs, to which I was rather partial. If you stuck one inside your cheek it could last for ages.

Uncle Harry was our favourite; he bore a striking resemblance to Harold Macmillan, though shorter, and he had twinkly grey eyes. He escaped the aggravating, illogical chatter of the women by working outside in the gardens and large orchard. Sometimes he would slip a honey comb into our bag, and I still remember the taste of his crunchy heather honey on home-baked brown bread.

They had all inherited family money; there was much discussion about its destination after their death, and the solicitor was regularly called to make changes to their instructions. But Uncle Harry, the first to go, was the one who remembered us, his legacy changing our lives for ever.

We were surrounded by interesting old characters, but the nearest lived at the mill, which by then had stopped functioning, only generating electricity for the lighting in their house, a pretty stone cottage with roses growing round the door.

A few yards beyond our house the tarred road came to an end with an ancient pack-horse bridge over a small river we called a 'beck', the Old Norse for 'stream', which led to the mill cottage and a cluster of outbuildings, some extended over time but all in the same beautiful local stone. There had been a mill there since medieval times but the present buildings were 18th and 19th century.

This was a busy time for the miller, when farmers, using horse and cart, delivered their own grain – oats and barley and later wheat – to be ground into meal and flour. Unfortunately, with the import of grain from abroad, enormous mills had sprung up in the large ports which affected trade in local mills until in the 1930s, only animal feed was produced here.

The couple who inhabited the mill most of the time we lived there were Hannah and John, both characters in their own right. Hannah inherited the mill from her father, Ned, who, apart from being a miller, played the violin at lively dances held in an extension of the inn in the village. After her father's day Hannah closed off the out buildings and installed a generator on one of the two wheels, thus becoming the first house in the village to have electricity – of sorts. In summer and at times when the water was low, I remember the light being weak and wavery, necessitating the use of oil lamps and candles like the rest of us.

The had both suffered misfortunes. Hannah wore a glass eye for reasons we never knew: a little shinier than her own but a reasonable match, and her face that was fixed in a perpetual beam. She only rarely visited the shop but would appear if you were passing her cottage on a walk up the fell, eager for a chat. She would sometimes break a sprig from a shrub called *Lad's Love,* growing by their front door in her small garden, crush it between her fingers and hold it by my nose. If I wrinkled it and made 'ugh' noises she would erupt into peals of laughter for at least a minute.

Her husband John had an artificial leg, which he negotiated with difficulty because the amputation had been at his upper thigh. He was the communicator of the two, and liked to discuss the old times. Mum told me he was a wise old bird. They were an intensely private couple, suspicious of strangers and anyone who might harm the water wheels, but they were kind and very fair. In summer he would come for his newspaper and lean over the counter and ask in a low conspiratorial voice, 'Ready for some more 'barb Mary?'

'Oh, yes please, John.'

And he would return with a large armful of beautiful pink rhubarb.

Each year, in June, John would wait till the shop was empty, and whisper in my mother's ear, 'Can you cancel the papers for three weeks, please Mary.'

'Right, John. Going somewhere nice?'

'Isle of Wight,' or 'Penzance' or 'the Isle of Skye,' or 'the Devon coast'; always somewhere far away,

Hannah and John by their water mill

showing a spirit of adventure unusual for the times. The unspoken message was that my mother should not mention their absence to anyone.

Then on the Saturday, in order to catch the 2 o'clock bus, John would set off first, at 1.30pm, and, leaning heavily on his stick, hobbled down the road in his best herring-bone suit and tweed cap, mackintosh draped over his shoulder. Ten minutes later, his wife, flushed of cheek, would follow with a suitcase in each hand, her dark fitted coat reaching to the ankles, plaits coiled in a bun, back straight and determined, joining her husband at the bus.

On their return, John would recount to my mother stories of places they had visited, scenery they had passed through, of boat trips to far-flung islands with the sense of wonderment of a true explorer.

Although the mill was no longer in working order, it was still kept scrupulously clean. Once my mother was given the honour of being shown round the interior of the old buildings, and was impressed to see that John tidied, swept and dusted all the rooms regularly. 'Like a new pin,' she said. He also guarded the two water wheels with his life. On one occasion he was incensed to find a local public schoolboy actually swinging on one of the wheels. The boys were given a free day out of school each summer to go off walking and amuse themselves as they saw fit - just asking for trouble, John remarked. So from that time on, having checked on the date of this annual exeat, from early morning to evening he stationed himself on a chair on the bridge, walking stick in hand, on guard, thus preventing further vandalism.

He also took up his post as sentry when my mother was white-washing the exterior of our house, which she did every three years in the month of May. As the house was three storeys high, long ladders were needed which we borrowed from the farm. She was not normally an early riser but loved a project, and, having checked the weather forecast, she rose at 6am for a breakfast of tea, bread and honey (also from the farm, and from heather – the best) assembled her tools and positioned the ladder, enjoying every minute. 'There is nothing so lovely as being high up a ladder on a sunny May morning, birds singing, a view of the fells...'

She never wore protective gear but simply turned her blouse and skirt inside out and wore an old pair of shoes, a brilliant idea that caused great amusement. Occasionally John would limp down over the bridge and, with Benger's help, check on the safety of the ladder, sometimes steadying it for a while. 'Careful, Mary,' he would murmur from time to time.

When I was very small I was intrigued by an elderly farmer who lived in the upper part of the valley, He was tall and thin with an untidy whiskery beard, and was known to everyone as Long John. His accent was very broad and you could say that he had never moved with the times. One day in the 1920s my great aunt Mary was walking through the fields with a friend (we were a family of Marys, the great aunt was Big Mary, my mother Little Mary, and I also was Mary but fortunately used my second name, possibly escaping the title of Tiny Mary). She was carrying her new box camera, probably hoping to catch a few artistic shots, when they met Long John wandering down the lane towards them, holding a pet lamb. He stopped and after a brief, 'Afternoon', he stared at the camera, fascinated.

''as ter gitten yan o' them pottygraphyin' machines?' he asked at last, poking his nose close to camera. Cameras had been around for a while, but Long John had obviously never encountered one. I like to think Auntie Mary took his photo and presented him with the snapshot but never heard the outcome of the encounter; this was a family fireside story that never changed with the telling.

But by far the best known eccentric of the village was our old lady, Mrs Martin, ('Auld Lily'), with her fluffy white hair, shins scabbed from sitting too near the fire and the black shapeless garments she favoured. Widowed for many years, she spent a great part of her adult life in a place she hated,

'I can't stand all these mountains,' she would declare, 'I'd like to *push* them over!'

Her enduring dream was to return to her home town of Maryport, a small dockland and mining settlement on the Cumbrian coast, but without close family and only a dog for company, she remained forever manacled to her stamps, postal orders, fishing licences and pensions, destined to die amongst her cursed mountains, though lucky to be cared for so well for the last years of her life.

Perhaps for this reason she grew even more cantankerous in her old age, viewing everyone with an air of deep suspicion. When, during the war, a gentleman asked her the name of the village she delivered her beady stare.

'I can't tell you that!'

'Why on earth not?' he asked.

'Because you might be a German spy!'

She held a fierce determination never to run out of anything, so, if someone asked for half a dozen two-pence-halfpenny stamps she would enquire, 'What did you do with the ones you got yesterday?'

Once, a local Lord who owned a house up the bank behind the village, politely requested a particular denomination of stamp.

'Sorry, don't have any,' she said firmly.

Leaning over the counter he caught sight of that particular page in her stamp book.

'Yes you have! Look!' he said, pointing.

'You're not having *that*, it's my last one.' And the matter was closed.

She was no respecter of persons. One day Professor Joad, philosopher and radio personality popular for his regular appearances on *Brains Trust*, had

the misfortune to enter her shop. Having put him in
his place over some purchase, he became very cross.

'Don't you know who I am?' he bellowed.

'You could be the King of England for all I care,'
she replied. 'You're only a man and a jolly rude one at
that!'

The story of this abrupt dismissal of a famous
person who appeared to be rather grand was much
enjoyed by the locals, every word being authenticated
by other customers present at the time.

Many years earlier, when going through that
difficult time of life, one summer morning Mrs
Martin was not present to open the post office at 9am.
Gradually a small crowd began to gather, the postman
delivering the morning mail, the paper man, milkman
and various nosy customers, one of them being my
great aunt who lived at the farm opposite. In spite of
knockings at the door and urgent calls of, 'Hello there!
Are you all right?' there was silence from within.

Finally, as fears for her state of health were
beginning to be voiced, the window of her attic
bedroom was thrown wide open and a dishevelled
head appeared and glared down at them.

'What's going on down there? What's all the
commotion?'

Then slowly with reluctance and some
resentment, Mrs Martin deigned to appear and begin
her day's work.

She had the misfortune to be hard of hearing,

so made periodic visits to see if there were customers waiting; to hear the familiar slip-slop of her slippers on the stone flags of her passage was always a relief. If you were unlucky enough to enter the shop immediately following a check, you might have a considerable wait. Once an 'off comer' had the temerity to complain.

'I've been standing here for ten minutes!' he said.

'You can stand there all year if you like,' she snapped. 'I'm not here to serve the likes of you, only the local people!'

To which there was no possible answer.

But my mother always said that beneath all the crustiness lay rather a sweet, amusing old lady. As I was born in the cottage next door to the post office my mother would frequently pop in for a chat or to help out if needed. Often, as the old lady did not look after herself very well, consuming large quantities of Pom, a kind of powdered potato mixed with water which appeared during the war and was often likened to glue, we would take her a Sunday dinner of meat, vegetables, gravy and real mashed potato which she consumed with relish; even after she had taken to her bed, she retained a healthy appetite.

There were skilled craftsmen in the valley including two woodcarvers, one of whom lived at the top of a steep bank by an old mill, his beard and moustache perpetually stained with nicotine. He made small pieces of furniture: boxes, candlesticks and other decorative items which have stood the test of time. The other old gentleman carved small animals and birds popular with the early visitors; sadly, he used unseasoned wood resulting in splitting after a few months, but they somehow managed to retain their charm in spite of the cracks.

Lower down the valley lived John, a cobbler who patiently dealt with all out footwear and the special request to have my brogues built up on the heel to compensate for my flat feet, always on the last day of the school holidays. He came from a family of six, the youngest of whom was Lance (Salkeld) Porter, born in 1911. In his short life Lance produced a wealth of prose and poetry, describing his stunning Cumbrian surroundings and country life before machinery took over. He was also involved in the establishing of the Lakeland Dialect Society, organising 'Merry Neets' when people of all walks of life met up to chat, sing and recite poetry in the Cumbrian dialect. He was a man of tremendous talent and potential whose career was cruelly cut short in 1943 when he 'Died of fever' aged 31 while serving in the Royal Corps of Signals in Iraq. One example of his poetry was singled out and included in *The Penguin Book of First World War Poetry* and the words of this moving poem are engraved on a large slab of slate attached to a wall of the parish church in valley.

All are now long gone, only alive in the memories of those who knew them. But their words and old ways still hang over the cottages and farmsteads scattered round the valley, over rivers where they fished and fields and meadows where they toiled, digging, ploughing and making hay.

In the churchyard, date, name and abode are recorded, and the rest is in the breath of the wind over the fells.

Grieve Not

If I should pass beyond man's thought, grieve not..
For He who plans the pattern of the stars,
Who sets each leaf on every tree and bush,
Knows of my course....
And if He will my destiny be life,
That life I seek... If death
Then death is but a gate to truth
Wider than all the sky, and more immense
Than all the universe.

Lance Salkeld Porter, June 1941

Boot church and churchyard

CHAPTER FIVE

A Grand Day

T IS the mingling of smells I remember; the damp grass, crushed by an army of boots, the muskiness rising from the sheep pens, and most of all the aroma of pipe tobacco smoke, rising up into the air from under flat tweed caps, a warm masculine smell of which I was lately deprived.

The date of our annual show was as immovable as the granite in the fells above, the last Saturday in September. Its purpose was originally to show, compare and judge the ancient breed of Herdwick sheep, said to have been introduced into the valleys by Norsemen a thousand years ago. But there was much more to our show than sheep.

Left: The Eskdale Show at Boot

On our return to school after the summer holiday, it was something we eagerly anticipated weeks ahead. We began to practise for the handwriting competition which was part of the show, a short set piece which, in the first year after my father's death, was, 'Love me love my dog.' With our dip pens, tongues protruding, we laboured over endless bits of paper, littered with inky blots and smudges.

'Oh, do it in pencil!' said our exasperated teacher at last. I do not remember any of us ever winning.

There was also a competition in the children's section for the best button-hole collected in the wild. With much enthusiasm I picked thistle flowers, sprigs of hazel-nuts and rowan berries, pieces of fern and any wild flowers left untouched by the frost. I tied their stems with wool and mounted them onto a piece of white card, admiring the results mightily, until I saw the other entries, elaborate, grand, and redolent of flower-arranging classes and WI lectures. Never mind, my big moment was yet to come.

The show was held in a field near the village in the heart of the fells, a scamper away from our house. On the evening before, our excitement escalated as we saw, with much hammering and shouting, the marquees being erected in the large field the other side of the beck. In the morning handicrafts were laid out on trestle tables for judging, and wagons unloaded sheep of all shapes and sizes, guided into pens by officious sheep-dogs. A bar from the local pub was erected in the largest tent, and the clinking of bottles echoed in the chilly air. We children watched, poked our noses into places we were not wanted, and chased up and down the field playing tig and leap-frog. At midday I wandered home for something to eat and to have my face scrubbed, hair combed and re-plaited, and to put on my best jumper and skirt.

Leaving our parents to follow later, we children made for the sheep, segregated into their enclosures, continually pushing, shoving and bleating.. The tups were belligerent, curly-horned shaggy lions with pale wide-set eyes. They butted the fence and each other, and sometimes one got out of control, and we longed for it to escape and run round the field charging everyone and causing havoc, but a farmer would appear and grab him from behind, sinking his fingers into the thick woolly fleece, and peace would be restored. We studied the labels: tups, gimmers, shearlings and twinters.

'Twinters?' we non-farmers giggled.

'Lived through two winters,' a man in an itchy-looking herringbone suit informed us. I liked the gimmer shearlings, fluffy young girls, clean and gentle as they huddled together waiting hopefully for their rosettes.

I would link arms with my friends and make for the handicraft tent. After a quick check on our spurned entries, we wandered past the Arran sweaters, matinée coats, knitted toys and cushion covers; then we sniffed and licked our lips over the Victoria sponges and currant pasty (cut in squares). Then someone would say, 'Let's get practising!' And we would run off to a quiet part of the field to prepare for what was, to me, the highlight of the day.

I was fortunate in being born with an ability to run – fast. No one could catch me, my father, mother, or even the older boys at school who would dangle a worm, shouting, 'Coming!' when I knew the intended destination was the back of my neck. I screamed obligingly, but secretly knew there was no risk of capture. I loved running, with the wind in my face and the world rushing by, streaming down the field with the pack behind me. And I knew that soon my purse would be full.

I practised the three-legged race with my friend Hazel, also a fast runner. We chanted 'ONE two, ONE two ONE two', stamping down our bound feet on the 'ONE', which sometimes worked and sometimes saw us tripping and crashing on top of each other. The sack race was a tricky one: did you shove your feet into the corners of the sack, or did you bunny jump for the whole race? I usually opted for both but lost time in the change-over. And did you cheat a tiny bit in the egg and spoon?

For the flat race our parents gathered by the side of the imaginary track, and two judges stood at the end stretching out a piece of string for the finish.

'On your marks!' Words to chill the spine.

'Get set! GO!' Then, with a spring forward, head back, heart in its proper place, my legs took over, and I did not even have to think, I just ran with a wild elation coursing through me. At the other end, after I had breasted the string, my mother would give me a big hug, and, although I did not say anything, I wished Daddy could have seen me.

The rewards were considerable. The first prize for a flat race was around seven shillings and sixpence, with a little less for the other races. I would always end up with a lovely pink ten-shilling note and lots of silver. We spent it on sweets, chocolate, bottles of fizzy lemonade and dandelion and burdock. And ice-cream. We ran to the van impatient for this creamy delicious treat. It was produced by a local dairy farmer, and if you had a wafer, the bottom biscuit was thicker, made of chocolate and marshmallow. During the day I probably managed four or five of them, with no ill effects, some of them paid for by generous uncles. And I always managed to save part of the winnings for my money-box.

There followed a lull in proceedings when we just mooched around. We would admire the hand-carved shepherds' crooks with horn handles, or watch the sheep dogs and terriers in the ring having their teeth inspected. We girls held hands or arms and the boys followed in untidy cavorting groups. We were always on the look out for the illicit, the untoward and the shocking. Like small, under-cover secret police, we watched and waited. It made our day if we spotted a man relieving himself against a tree, or discovering a couple kissing behind a trailer.

'And they're both married to other people!' one of the boys once remarked in disgust.

Sometimes we might happen upon two farmers having a beer-fuelled argument over grazing rights, with the air trembling with forbidden words. We hung around for a while in the hope of a fight which never materialised. A truck stuck in the mud or a tent blowing over were amusing incidents, when a pugnacious bucking animal and a snarling dog definitely had potential. And of course, much of the action took place around the beer tent, voices and laughter increasing in decibels as the day progressed. We were on the alert for unsteady gait, and news spread round our army like lightning if someone fell over, eyes crossed, smiling at the sky.

'Come and look at Bobby. He's kettled!' and we would gather round fascinated, scrutinising him closely.

Everything was allowed because it was show day.

Hound trailing is a Lakeland sport bordering on obsession. A rag dipped in aniseed and paraffin is dragged round a course of 8 to 10 miles to make a trail up the fells and back to the show field. Owners and hounds line up at the start, as wild howling fills the air. In those years the all-time champion hound was Perivale: in one season he won fifty-eight races.

I felt loosely related to him, as he was owned by my great-great Uncle Jack, and was trained by my father's brother, John, who provided him with raw eggs and sherry and sixteen miles of exercise each day during the season, eight in the morning and eight at night. Uncle John would appear in the afternoon, pull one of my plaits and say, 'Hello Pat. How are ye doin'?'

I would blush deeply and reply, 'All right thank you,' but secretly I was proud that this tall dark man with eyes the colour of river pebbles was my uncle.

At the call, the hounds were released and bounded off to leap over streams, climb walls and rocky crags and cross moorland. Soon, all you could see were white specks moving in the heather and plunging through bracken.

'Ay. It's a fine sight,' everybody said.

The bookies called out the odds and people placed last-minute bets. After half an hour someone would spot a hound, binoculars would be raised, and the faint clamour of the dogs sounded in the distance. Tension mounted. Then there began a cacophony which had to be heard to be believed: screaming, piercing whistles, clanging of bells, shouting of names till the atmosphere was so electric you would not dare to light a match, and goose-pimples came up on the back of your neck, even as a child. The hounds arrived on the home straight, tongues lolling, loped to the finish and ran straight to their owners, astonishingly recognising their own calls above all the din.

'Good lad, good, lad,' they said, and made a tremendous fuss of the panting dogs. We stood by and watched, fascinated.

This was a social day for families and friends, an opportunity to meet up and exchange news. The women stood in their warm coats or waterproofs and head-scarves tied under the chin, holding cardboard cups of tea, while many of the men disappeared to have a crack over a pint. All over the field you heard comments like:

'Hello, Elsie. Haven't seen you for ages.'

'When's her operation?'

'Ay, things aren't so good between them.'

'Sad news about Joe.'

Much ground had to be covered in a short time; it felt like a big party with non-stop refreshments.

Later in the afternoon, as the temperature dropped and shadows lengthened, everyone gathered round the ring for the competitions, starting with the Cumberland wrestling. Traditional dress for this sport was a pair of long-johns, vest, and brief pants on top.

'OK lads,' the commentator said, 'tek hod,' which meant take hold in the starting position. After some walking around they would burst into action; three throws and it was over and the next couple came forward. We enjoyed it at first, but with no injuries and too many competitors we lost interest, and were impatient for the next event to start, which was the horn-blowing.

The horn in question was the hunting horn, and it seemed as though only a couple of people had any experience of ever blowing it. The have-a-goers were painful.

'Blimey,' someone would say, 'sounds like our cow calving.'

The hallowing competition was more enjoyable. You walked into the ring, had your three goes, and made room for the next. The announcer, who kept us entertained throughout the day with his cryptic comments, would say things like, 'Thank you, Jack. Keep practising!'

One year my mother looked round and was surprised to see me standing on the box in the middle of the ring, with my hands cupped round my mouth, facing the fell for maximum echo. I had been preparing for this moment for weeks.

'Haaa-hooo!' I went, three times. My voice floated over to the fell opposite, then returned. I was magnificent. I outshone them all.

I think I was awarded fourth place, though they only paid out on three. The winner was quite poor, in my opinion.

The crowds by this time were gradually thinning, the light was softening, warming the bronze tints of the bracken on the fell behind, and we children, tired after the day's activities, hunted down our parents and hung on to their arms or sat on their knees. The last event of the day was Mum's and my favourite: the singing.

There were three categories in this section, comic, hunting and sentimental. Entries for the comic were fewer, and they tended to have naughty words; consequently sometimes singers had to be stopped in the middle. Hunting songs were next, but in this class the entrants were often missing.

'Next, Jim Jenkins,' called the announcer. Silence.

'Anybody seen Jim?'

'Ay. He's in t'beer tent.' Laughter all round.

Finally Jim would make an appearance, reluctant and rosy faced, protesting he had consumed too much beer to sing, but he was ushered into the ring anyway. Lakeland hunting songs were much-loved, sung in the pubs after a long day's hunting and a tatie-pot supper. Because of their length, the singer had to be restricted to six verses, but one old man always refused to leave, and had to be firmly escorted out of the ring; you could still hear strains of verse 13 as he wobbled his way back to his pint.

'Any more entries for the sentimental?'

There were two or three lads with pure tenor voices, untrained but with the natural talent to hold a tune. Scottish and Irish songs were popular, and in-keeping with the setting. Our favourites were *The Rose of Tralee* and *I'll Take You Home again, Kathleen*. The singer would grasp the microphone, lift his chin and let his voice soar, lingering on the high notes. The sound rang out over the hills, and the crowd would fall silent. At the end there would be a collective 'ah' of appreciation followed by loud applause and whistling.

By then it would have grown cold, with dusk falling. Car engines started up, dogs were deposited in the back, and people turned their faces homeward. Memories of that first year without my father stay in my mind, wandering back slowly down the road while I told Mum about my day. I yawned. I had been awake since six. A few pale stars had appeared above the fell behind our house. We met a neighbour, cap tilted over his eyes, cigarette glowing in the half light. He was off to the pub to continue the festivities.

'Grand day, lasses,' he murmured, without removing his cigarette.

'Yes,' we replied, 'a grand day.'

CHAPTER SIX

Moving On

HE summer following my father's death was a sunny one, which was fortunate, as it was decided that my mother should take on the job of covering for the postman over his annual three week leave, and the whole of the round was on foot. On some days I accompanied her. We started in the village, delivering to a scatter of houses and a couple of farms, cycled to the other side of the valley and, leaving our bikes at the bottom, puffed our way up a fell for two and a half miles to a holiday cottage and three remote farm houses. But each stop was not just a delivery.

'Owt fresh?' the farmer's wife would inquire. There then followed a brief résumé of the latest news from the village, at the relating of which my mother was adept: deaths, new babies, sudden illnesses or marriages were all discussed over a cup of tea and a wedge of cake, and a few incredulous '*No!*'s. The journey back was glorious, with the whole of the Scafell range stretched out before us, blue and mysterious. We rarely met a soul, and I still hear the bubbling song of the skylarks above our heads, and the hiss of the waterfall as we descended the hill, hurrying home for a late lunch.

As summer approached, the nagging time began.

'When can I go into white socks, Mum?

'When the last snow has gone off Scafell.' No arguing with that.

'Can I wear summer dresses now? It's *boiling*.'

'*Please* can I go bathing? The others are going.'

There were pools in the river close by, small and rocky, sometimes only waist deep, but any time there was a glimmer of sun we were off across the field with our old faded bathing suits, and would leap into the glassy surface, and plunge to the bottom head-first like squawking ducks, chasing minnows and retrieving stones from the green underworld. We stayed in the water till our teeth chattered and our skin was translucent, and had to play chasing games till we were warm again. Rarely supervised.

I had the good fortune to be born towards the end of July, so my party was often a picnic by the river; the place where we swam is now cordoned off, considered to be too dangerous for access due to a whirlpool further down. It was a perfect site, a good-sized pool and a long stretch of volcanic rock, smoothed away through the ages, where you could tuck in a hollow and chew your sandwich in comfort. My mother would sit back on a cushion reading *The News Chronicle* while we played.

'Mum, look at me! Look at me!'

'Mrs Nolan! Pat's doing dangerous things!'

'Mmm,' she would say absently, still reading the paper, 'be careful.' Then when she finally looked up, 'Get down off there, now!'

Shortly after school finished in the summer, there would be a knock at our door.

'Arthur's started hay-timin'. Are ye cumin'?

The farmer who owned the field opposite always needed help, and, with chins resting on the stone wall, we watched him lead his horse and mowing machine up and down, slicing through swathes of long juicy stems. Then we children, half a dozen of us, were allowed to enter and take one of the wide wooden rakes and spread out the grass to dry. Over the days we raked it into long rows, then into small hay-cocks, and finally into tall stacks. The smell of the drying hay permeated the air round us, musty and sweet, mingling with the murmur of voices and the swallows twisting and darting overhead. No larking about was allowed or we were sent home. At lunch time the farmer took out a flask of tea and his bait box and we nipped home to collect a sandwich, and if we were lucky, a bottle of lemonade, and sat on the prickly ground, knees bent, leaning against a stack, munching and enjoying the peace and the sun on our skin. Sometimes we were thrown a few toffees as a reward for our labours. Finally, on the last day, the farmer would appear in the morning with his horse and cart.

'Time for leading,' he said gruffly, which meant forking as much hay onto the cart as was safe, and we, delirious with excitement, sat precariously on the top while the old horse plodded across the next field to the barn. It took most of the day to clear the meadow, and in the barn we jumped and rolled on the high bank of hay to pack it down, on the golden stalks and skeletons of clover, red campion and daisies, and squealed as much as we wanted. In the evening, ravenous for my tatie-pot supper, I would return home, brown and dusty, and as I undressed for a wash, hay seeds trickled onto the floor from under my plaits and out of my clothes and shoes.

'Worse than an old farmer,' my mother remarked.

In September, something very wonderful happened; we had an addition to the family. My uncle, who owned kennels and bred gun dogs, offered us a young cocker spaniel that had survived a bout of distemper but was left with a slight limp in his back leg and so could not be shown. He was a pedigree whose full name was Mount Close Benger, and his colour was officially 'blue roan', black with grey and white markings. He arrived late one Saturday afternoon, miserable and shaking having been sick in the van every half hour since they left home in Essex. He refused to eat or even look at us, but lapped a little water and pined. He was achingly beautiful, with large soulful eyes and black silky ears, and I adored him on sight. Gradually we found him to be playful, loving and loyal, but very jealous; any child my mother hugged was a marked target, and elicited ominous growling from under the table. He and I became inseparable.

Unless it snowed, or froze so hard we could skate on small ponds and tarns, we were not too keen on winter, and seemed to be perpetually cold. Normally a house had only one source of heat which was an open fire in the main room. Our cottage had a black Victorian range, with grate, oven, a small boiler for heating water (which did not work) and a hob at the side for a kettle or pan. With no electricity, most of the cooking and baking took place here, with a primus stove as a back-up.

By the evening the heat had built up, and these were the cosiest times for me. The curtains would be drawn, the Tilley lamp lit, fuelled by paraffin and pumped to give a strong light, then placed on the table. An oil lamp would sit in the corner behind what used to be my father's chair, and a shovel of coal and a couple of logs were thrown on the fire. I would be at the table in the pool of light reading or doing a crossword in my comic, Mum knitting or working on a rag rug. Occasionally cinders dropped from the fire into the ash underneath, the most comforting sound you could ever imagine.

At bedtime, it was a cold wash in the kitchen or possibly a sluice down in a zinc bath in front of the fire, using kettles of hot water. Then a candle was lit and carried upstairs to a freezing bedroom, where, amidst the quivering shadows, the nightly check for witches and wolves took place, and then into an icy bed, with a stone hot water bottle if the weather was particularly raw.

Sometimes friends of my mother would arrive later and make up a four for whist, after which she made a hot drink and they sat talking for hours. I used to listen to the rise and fall of voices and the occasional burst of laughter, and wonder how they found enough to talk about. But in those days topics were discussed and sifted, old times revisited and amusing incidents related. Conversation was an art and an entertainment which everyone had to learn, or they made poor company. There was no competition from television, and the radio was only switched on for certain programmes: the news, a comedy show or music for my mother, who in the mornings sang along to the latest songs in a dreadful voice.

Then, in February, when there was no work around and we were trying to eke out the widow's pension, our life suddenly changed; the old lady at the post office in the village fell and broke her wrist. My mother, being friendly with her, helped out, and during that time a plan was made between them: we would buy the house at a lower price if my mother looked after her for the rest of her days. At seventy-eight, with a mass of unkempt white hair, she was an eccentric character about whom many stories circulated, mostly related to her forthright and contentious disposition, but my mother liked her and recognised that behind her crusty exterior lay a keen sense of humour.

The idea was that we would borrow the money from a wealthy aunt, but shortly before the deal was finalised, a great uncle died leaving us a legacy which would pay for the house and its renovation. The relief to my mother was enormous. Sadly, the week after we moved into the house, Mrs Martin fell, broke her hip and took to her bed, never to leave it again, thus doubling the amount of work involved.

The house was a large three storey Victorian building of painted brick, with a row of cottages attached to one side and an ancient barn to the other. Entering it for the first time, Benger and I ran amok, up one set of stairs to the attics, and back down another, through four bedrooms on the first floor and three on the second. After the small cottages we had occupied, this was a palace, though in size only. There was no electricity, but worse, no water laid on, so trips to fetch our household water from the beck twenty yards away had to be made with a bucket in each hand, lethal in icy weather. Clandestine visits were made every few days to tip the lavatory bucket into the beck, a few yards down from our watering hole, naturally. The roof leaked in several places, windows needed replacing, damp patches decorated the walls, there were no cooking facilities other than an open fire, and the whole place was overrun by mice, to whom Mrs M. was rather partial, leaving little heaps of crumbs out for them at night.

'What have I taken on?' cried my mother, looking heavenwards. 'An invalid, a child, a dog and a house that's falling down around my ears!'

But the saving grace was the garden, once it was cleared of weeds and raspberry canes. At the back it was paved, with shrubs at the edge, but if you walked round behind the outside lavatory, there was a secret garden with a low wall separating it from a field, with uninterrupted views to the mountains. A lawn was seeded and a large number of old-fashioned rose bushes planted, and any visitor who came in the summer was presented with a fragrant armful of pink, yellow and crimson.

It was Easter time when we moved in, a time of hope and rebirth. Lambs cavorted in the field behind the house, the tree holding our washing line was sprouting pale pink blossom, a few rogue daffodils were pushing through the weeds and on the fell, the gorse bushes were in full bloom, excellent news for us Pace Egg dyers. Preparation was imperative: in the collection of onion skins, gorse flowers and of course fresh eggs, preferably not brown. The results were always unexpected but often very beautiful and the Pace Eggs gave a celebratory touch to our arrival at

Dale View, the official name for our house, though not often used. The eggs sat in the family rum butter bowl glowing a rich mahogany colour until we could eat them on Easter Sunday.

The arrival of a ginger tom called Tosca soon solved the mouse problem, much to the old lady's disgust, and gradually the house was made habitable and weather-proof. Water arrived, followed later by electricity, and we experienced great excitement at the fitting of our first bathroom, which, as a former bedroom, had a large sash window from which, whilst reclining in the bath in unaccustomed soapy luxury, you could admire the uninterrupted view of the fells through clouds of steam.

When we arrived at our new home, the tiny shop on the ground floor sold a small selection of sweets and newspapers, but gradually shelves were filled, new lines introduced, and over the years, business began to flourish.

And so it was that, owing to a small accident, our lives were transformed and we were happy and secure in our new home Our old lady died peacefully in her bed after two and a half years, having developed a deep affection for Benger which sadly was never reciprocated; whenever he was put in her room, he sat and stared at the door till my mother returned. Tosca, the cat, however, often slept in the crook of her neck and licked her face till it took on an unhygienic shine, which she adored.

Living in a sweet shop offered constant temptation, but it was the people from different places and different strata of society who fascinated me, and our little shop was a melting pot. And the situation of the village was perfect: a cul-de-sac beside the river with an old bridge and Elizabethan water mill the other side, from which a path ran up to a steeply rising fell. In the evenings hikers would return with their enormous rucksacks, stop to buy refreshments, and, if it was warm we sat out at the front chatting to them about their day and their lives. We listened with interest, but never for a moment wished to change places with them, to abandon a busy life in the shop, our twilight walks at the end of a day, and supper in the garden looking out to the hills, breathing in the scent of the roses.

Herdwick sheep

CHAPTER SEVEN

Jack's Bus

 CAN see it now, parked in the village, cream and green paintwork polished to a waxy shine, its rounded contours homely, windows white with reflected light and door flung open in readiness for the forthcoming trip. A row of distant fells lie behind; nearer, copses of silver birch and an occasional oak or sycamore.

This chugging ponderous vehicle served as our means of escape from the valley to far-flung places, bigger villages than ours on the coastal plain, and most exciting of all, to the grand metropolis of Whitehaven, where everything we could possibly need was available, at a price. There was one trip per day to different destinations, but Thursdays and Saturdays it was to

Whitehaven, chosen as those were the market days. It used to be an elegant Georgian town, but in later times was stripped of its former glory, and in these post-war days it looked distinctly shabby. Not that we cared.

We would all arrive at the bus with a few minutes to spare, with faces scrubbed, fresh hair ribbons, and mothers powdered and lipsticked with a dab of 'Evening in Paris' behind the ears.

'Hello, Jane. Hello Kathleen, how's the leg?' My mother would do the social bit, then we would choose ourselves a seat half-way down the bus. Five minutes before take-off Jack, the owner/driver would appear from his house and waddle over to the bus, dark grey jacket and waistcoat stretched over a capacious stomach and with his cap surgically attached to his forehead.

'Afternoon.' Delving into a black shoulder bag he would distribute tickets and drop the money into it with a chink.

'Everybody 'ere?' There would follow a short discussion as to who might be intending to come, and sometimes a matronly figure could be spotted hurrying up the road, basket over arm.

'Sorry Jack. Mi clock must be slow,' and pink-faced with exertion and embarrassment she would collapse into a seat and we were off.

We picked up passengers on the way, at the end of farm tracks, beside banks of high willow-herb, where there might be an elderly couple looking expectant, and at various villages en route. The journey of twenty miles took at least an hour, the first part being winding and hilly. Jack had an excellent driving record, mainly because he went at a snail's pace. Only once did we have an accident. When passing through a built up area, the brakes failed, and, with a strong smell of burnt toast, we veered off abruptly to the left and found ourselves teetering over someone's geranium bed. The lady owner ran out, eyes bulging and mouth open in an O shape, though we could hear no sound. Nobody was hurt or had moved, except me. I skidded down the aisle to the front of the bus and arrived by Jack's left elbow. He turned his head to look at me, his normally ruddy face the colour of a grocer's shop candle, and seemed surprised to find me wrapped around the gear stick.

'You a' reet?'

'Yes, thank you.' I stood up to find that I was: only a small graze on my knee. As I returned to my seat plump sympathetic hands reached out to pat me.

'You didn't half go a cropper!'

I decided to milk it a bit, and started to rub my knee with little intakes of breath to indicate pain, with pleasing effect. When I arrived back to our seat, Mum said, 'Let's have a look,' and I showed her the grazed knee. She smiled. 'You'll live,' she said, and so ended my brief moment of martyrdom.

Fortunately we were rescued by another coach company, so our visit to town was not too curtailed, and we were able to do what we always did on arrival, and that was to head for the King Café, where we ordered meat and potato pie, rich brown gravy, large chips, peas and bread and butter, and rather than today's jug of tap water, we were brought an enormous pot of steaming hot tea.

The serious shopping then began. The highlight for me was a visit to The Beehive, Whitehaven's only department store. The toy section was in the basement, and I was always allowed to put a penny in the metal laughing-man's mouth, which made him chortle away for all of a minute, while my mother leafed through the clothes racks upstairs. We could not afford toys unless it was Christmas or my birthday, but I enjoyed browsing and planning ahead. The shop had a unique way of taking payment: the bill with our money was placed into a metal canister which then whizzed up through a series of pipes to some secret destination. A minute later it would miraculously come shooting back with the receipt and our change, always correct.

Jack timed our departure to allow a visit to first house pictures. There were three cinemas to choose from. My first film, at the age seven, was *Little Women* and I remember crying into Mum's sleeve when Beth died. Then, as Mario Lanza was a great favourite of hers, we saw *The Great Caruso* and *Because You're Mine*. Once again I cried when we began to realise that Caruso's sore throat was not merely a bad cold but Something Worse. Although they were adult films, it

was such a thrill to go to the cinema that we children never objected; it was a glimpse into other lives and other worlds which were a revelation to us.

Then it would be back to the bus with its leathery smell and the rectangular lights by each seat switched on. We compared our day and looked into our parcels, fingering, checking the colour, admiring. The suspension under us creaked and squeaked like an asthmatic pig, complaining about the bumps and twists in the road.

Towards home Jack would slow down, toot the horn and throw an evening paper into somebody's garden or by their door.

'Thanks Jack,' would float out a voice from within.

Sometimes he had a package to hand over, and towards the final stretch he would stop at a pub and switch off the engine.

89

'Parcel for t'*Rose and Crown*,' he announced.

Two pints later he returned.

And so it was with the next two pubs, the last stop being three pints long. He always came back with a piece of spicy news, a disaster or scandal of some sort, to deflect the wrath of disgruntled passengers.

'Big accident at Green Bank corner. Two dead.'

Or, 'Just heard, Jim Mason's run off with 'is sister-in-law.'

'Aye?' Someone would always fall for it and ask for more details and then a general discussion ensued over mutterings from the back. And at last, weary from our long day, we arrived home, kicked the fire into life and had a reviving mug of cocoa.

The bus was also used for visits to the doctor or the dentist, more often to the latter, as our GP routinely visited once a fortnight. Our dentist lived on the coast ten miles away, a forty minute journey. The extremes of pain one suffered in his chair would not be tolerated nowadays, but then it was considered a short if agonising alternative to perpetual toothache. Once, as the dentist was drilling he hit a nerve, and I pulled the drill from my mouth, to much cursing and shouting from him. He was generally respected, due to his imposing physique and cultured voice, a trust misplaced, as it emerged later.

One sunny June morning, aged nine, I set off for the bus in my favourite blue gingham dress and red ribbons at the end of my plaits. I had an appointment at the dentist for an extraction, but was on my own as my mother was busy with the post office by then. I did not mind, and giving Jack my money I chose a window seat, and, pressing my nose to the glass, waved to people walking in the road and watched the farmers raking up the hay – we had had a long spell of hot weather lately – and its warm musky smell filled the bus. I scanned the hedgerows and meadows for my favourite flowers: buttercups, red clover, tall foxgloves where you could poke you finger but never lick, and best of all Germander speedwell, which I loved for its name and tiny blue face poking out of the grass. As the ground flattened out my heart began to sink, and all too soon the bus came to a halt.

I was early, and dragging my feet, wandered up the hill towards the surgery.

'Sit down there. You'll have to wait a while,' said the receptionist, raising her pencilled eyebrows at me. Then she gave a little smile, and pointed to a pile of comics in the corner. She had beautiful hair, dark and curly all over, unlike my miserable, dead straight locks.

'Next please.' Dr. Brown emerged and ushered me into his chamber of horrors. He looked into my mouth, and injected me in two or three places in the gum with an industrial dose of cocaine.

'Do you know,' he said, peering into my mouth, 'the tooth next to it seems a bit suspect. I can take that out as well. OK?

'Ugh ugh,' I replied, in no position to object.

It was all over in minutes, and there was no pain. My left jaw and cheek were a frozen block, right up to the eye. Clutching a hankie Mum had given me, I walked back down the hill in a bit of a daze. At least I had not missed the bus home, something we had worried about. I spat into a bramble hedge and boarded the bus, which by now held around fifteen people.

But as I sat, I felt the good side of my mouth filling up with blood, and with lips pressed together, waited for the next stop, when I leapt out and discharged another scarlet mouthful on to a surprised colony of ants. This was repeated several times until Jack finally noticed.

'You a' right love?' he asked, laying a fatherly hand on my shoulder. Then, assessing the situation, said, 'You should get yourself some like mine,' and rattled a double set of grey porcelain gnashers at me.

At one point we travelled for over ten minutes without a stop. I felt my mouth fill up again, and glancing at my reflection in the window, thought I looked like a drawing of the north wind in children's picture books. We arrived home just in time.

Dr Brown's denouement created a quite a stir. One morning his patients arrived for their appointments to find the surgery locked up. It transpired that our dentist had eloped with his receptionist, and that not only was his title of Doctor a fake, but his dental qualifications were also bogus. Much was said in hindsight.

Our Sunday School trip was particularly exciting, as it took us to far-away places like Morecambe and, on one occasion, Blackpool. Children's requirements were simpler in those days: a wild chasing game on the sea-shore, sandwiches eaten outdoors, a tour around the shops to buy a couple of cheap souvenirs, a dip in the sea, and the best treat of all, a donkey ride across the sand. Some sunshine would be welcome but the weather was of secondary importance to us. And finally, we piled back on the bus and sank into our seats to play, and probably break, a little game we had bought. No pit-stops for Jack on these occasions. As we neared home, many of the younger ones would be asleep, and one or two of the mothers who were strong singers would start off a few songs, possibly of Vera Lynn fame, and we all joined in with the last one, *Now is the Hour for Me to Say Goodbye* which I loved and sang every word.

Then Jack would turn his head slightly.

'Put that cat out.' And we would see in the driving mirror that he was smiling.

Our school trip was less exotic, almost always to the nearest seaside village, but any escape from school was a bonus. The beach was pebbly and sandy when the tide was out. I do not think we went swimming but we were allowed to paddle. One time, I remember taking off my shoes and socks and placing them on the stones. They were my best shoes, which I had pestered to be allowed to wear, Start-Rite, the colour of conkers fresh from the shell, and built up a quarter of an inch on the heel, as it had been discovered I was suffering from the first stages of flat feet and knock knees. I tucked my dress into my knickers and ran off splashing through the white frills of sea screaming louder than the gulls overhead. Returning fifteen minutes later to collect my shoes, I found they had disappeared. I ran up and down panic-stricken searching for them, but in vain.

'They've been washed out to sea,' someone correctly suggested, and I stared out to the horizon hoping to spot two shiny shoes bobbing over the waves. Finally my friend Hazel lent me a pair of sand shoes a size too small, and I sat on the bus by the window, a huddle of misery, wondering what my mother would say.

I arrived at our front door which was open, saw my mother and burst into a deluge of tears.

'Whatever's the matter?' And then she saw my feet.

'Well, you'll just have to wear your old ones, won't you? We can't afford any more.' And somehow I wished she had screamed at me.

'Anyway, what was your teacher doing?'

'Reading the paper,' I replied. And felt a tiny bit better.

The bus was our life-line, an escape to a world of colour, excitement, bustle and noise, a far cry from our sleepy valley. And whole lives and episodes were played out during those journeys; news and gossip were exchanged, affairs started and ended, displays of affection took place on the back seat and friendships were forged. I learnt the whole of my tables on the bus, my father poking his head through the gap between the headrests and saying. 'Eight sixes – nine nines?' And I consumed a whole library of books.

But, ultimately, we were country people, and we were happy to return to the dale and to see the sun set over our mountains and fells, shadows constantly moving over the Herdwick sheep grazing on windswept moors, and to watch the last rays catch the roof of Jack's bus, parked outside his garage, in readiness for the next trip.

CHAPTER EIGHT

An Abundance of Holly

NCE we had picked all the ripe hazelnuts to put into store for winter, swished our way through banks of dry leaves and reduced Guy Fawkes to a smouldering heap, sparks and fragments of black ash flying heavenwards to appreciative shrieks, then our thoughts turned, with eager anticipation, to Christmas.

In the first years without my father, we had to devote much thought to producing gifts for friends and relations on a tiny budget. My mother worked on small rag rugs, begging hessian sacks from the coal man, washing them and marking out a design. Then old woollen clothes were colour-coded, snipped into short strips and pulled through the sacking with a special hook. Jokingly she once admired a coat of a rather fetching red colour belonging to a woman in the village, saying it would look perfect in one of her rugs. Eighteen months later we spotted the same person marching down the path to our cottage, red coat over her arm.

'There!' she said. 'That's for your rug.'

My mother also made leather purses, bags, and slippers for my girl cousins. My contributions to proceedings were books which I had been instructed to read neatly; those that had not been inscribed were then to be presented to other children. Usually I did not object as I practically knew the stories by heart, so long as fresh supplies arrived on Christmas Day. Using pinking shears I cut round bunches of Christmas roses, snowmen and skating scenes from old cards to make gifts tags, and, rescuing used pieces of wrapping paper which were free of holes and sticky tape, we would spend a cosy evening by the fire parcelling up our home-made presents.

Then the two cakes had to be baked, the second one being for my then unmarried uncle who was a gamekeeper in the border country and was not able to come home for the festivities. When the cakes were cool a liberal sprinkling of brandy was administered, then a layer of almond paste. Uncle John's cake was only given a topping of plain icing as it was to be posted, but on ours we went to town. Mum made a fancy edging, squirting small blobs of icing all the way round, just touching, and then it was my turn to arrange the ornaments, a motley bunch, consisting of a skier, a small fir tree, a tiny matrioshka doll, Santa Claus, a log cabin and a Bambi, until one of its legs broke off. Sometimes I made tiny footprints from one of the characters to the cabin – artistic licence here, as the house was half the size of the people. The finishing touch was a paper frill pinned around the cake, which was then stored away in a tin.

My mother prided herself on her mince-pies, made from something called rough puff pastry, rolled out six times with a few more knobs of butter added each time. They were quite delicious – crisp, with a shower of papery crumbs falling on your knee as you bit into them.

Rum butter was an annual treat and sometimes added to your mince pie, though we preferred it with plain biscuits or scones. I favoured our recipe, being more rummy and less sugary than that of our neighbours.

The atmosphere at school sweetened a little at the approach of Christmas. After our morning prayer – 'Hands together, eyes closed' – we would warble our way through a carol. My favourite was *In the Bleak Midwinter*, for the words, 'earth stood hard as iron, water like a stone' which sent tickles up my spine, and for its mournful tune. We decorated the school room, as functions would take place there after we had broken up. We twisted long chains of crepe paper in a variety of colours and our teacher pinned them up in the corners of the room; home-made bells and snowmen stood in window sills, and a fir tree appeared in the corner awaiting decoration.

One afternoon the wife of our local Lord appeared in her fur coat and a cloud of perfume with undertones of gin. They lived in London but spent most holidays in the valley. In her arms was a large box which said 'Harrods' on it. We all chanted, 'Thank you very much Lady --' and when our teacher opened the box we were transfixed; there lay a dozen baubles for our tree, so exotic and complicated the likes of which we had never seen before. Miss Jackson held one up and it sparkled with refracted light from our oil lamps and the fire in every colour of the rainbow, and when she turned it round I saw my face upside down in the back of it. With *oohs* and *ahs* they were hung from the tree and we were forbidden to touch them. On the last day of term when the tree was transferred to church, it was unanimous that the ornaments were not to be sent, but only our usual every-year ones instead.

'They would only break them,' said a boy, the same one who later that day put his thumb right through the middle of one of the more delicate baubles.

One year our teacher decided, rashly, that we would provide a Christmas entertainment for the parents and villagers. We arranged a tableau of the nativity, where I was Mary and swathed in a pair of old blue curtains. We posed for a few minutes feeling it was all rather odd, then lined up to give a rendition of some carols, which is where the afternoon began to deteriorate. Rehearsal time had been brief, and we forgot the words to the carols; some sang the first verse over again, and others simply made it up. Then, fatally, one of the boys laughed, and gradually everyone began to join in. Miss Jackson, seated at the piano with her back to the audience, turned purple, mouthing the words to us interspersed with 'Stop it!' and it was then I realised for the first time that even if you dislike someone, it is still possible to pity them, as I did then. She was humiliated in front of everyone, and for once could not smack us.

'I'm so sorry,' she was obliged to announce. 'Not enough rehearsal time, I'm afraid,' and as she turned, the look she cast in our direction did not bode well for Monday morning.

At home and in the church there was an abundance of greenery and holly, all gathered from hedgerows and woodlands nearby. On the last Sunday before Christmas our Carol Service was held, always well-attended. The nine readers, a mixture of young adults and children, were seated in the choir stalls, and after each person had read, they returned to the far end of the pew and everyone moved up one, so the torture of waiting was dripped slowly with each move, till, when my turn came, my stomach was inhabited by a cloud of moths. The vicar instructed us to wait till the penultimate verse of the carol, then walk to the lectern with its massive bible supported by the wings of a carved wooden eagle, find our place and wait until everyone had sat down and stopped coughing.

I read a lesson each year from the age of eight. The first time, I practised in church with my mother sitting at the back, calling, 'Slower, louder, louder still, not so fast!' till I knew the whole reading by heart.

'Now the birth of Jesus Christ was on this wise...' I piped up. It went off reasonably well if rather speedily, and post reading I was filled with such relief I threw back my head and sang the familiar carols with gusto. The candles on the altar flickered, the holly berries glowed, our voices soared and Mum smiled up at me from the congregation.

By Christmas Eve the air crackled with excitement down our row of cottages, and much discussion took place amongst the children about the presents we hoped to receive. We visited the only grocer's shop in the village for last-minute provisions, stuffed the chicken or goose which had been reared by us, and prepared the bread sauce. The whole house smelled of Christmas, of cloves, apple tree logs which we had bought to eke out the coal, and of secrets. A neighbour or two might call in for a glass of port or sherry and one of the mince pies that were warming by the fire. Then, once in my pyjamas, I organised Santa's drink of ginger wine and had a small snifter myself, an annual treat. Then it was off to bed, leaving a stocking and a pillow-case for my loot. I do not remember the point when I stopped believing in the old man, and if doubts crept in I ignored them; it was all part of the game.

But on Christmas morning, the year my father died, the day was damp and misty. My mother was busy downstairs lighting the fire, and I remember the presents being quite disappointing. I had to open them alone whilst listening to the raised voices of the four children next door:

'Look what I've got, look what I've got!' penetrated the thin dividing wall, as they tore into their wonderfully exciting presents. I received an annual which looked interesting, even if it was a year out of date, and a doll that said 'Mama' when you upended it, but some strange things rolled out of the promising shaped packets: a small bag of toiletries, with hard square things called bath cubes, which I found hard to imagine bobbing about in our tin bath by the fire once a week, and out of another parcel fell a hairbrush. What I really wanted was a tool set, penknives with lots of gadgets attached, a bow and arrow, a kite, games and of course lots of books.

No one played outside that day and no one visited. Mum must have missed Dad at those times, as I probably did, but neither of us mentioned him for fear of upsetting the other. We had lunch and later drew the curtains, switched on the radio and played a game together or did a jigsaw, and Mum fell asleep in the chair.

But when I was ten, for the first time I was allowed to attend the midnight service on Christmas Eve, by which time we had moved to the post office. We set off before eleven, as the service began at 11.30pm., walking down the mile-long, unmade road to our small stone- built church by the river, with a rocky fell rising up from the other side.

The service was popular. Chores had been completed, supper cleared away, and people were in mellow mood. Especially mellow were customers from the local pubs, who, feeling suddenly nostalgic and Christmassy, arrived noisily, parking their cars on the church green by the river. They walked in with sheepish nods and smiles, embarrassed perhaps at being thought religious, and the air was filled with spirit of the secular variety.

They particularly enjoyed the singing, and lingered over their favourite bits. Our teacher sat at the harmonium, not so much playing it as leaning on it squeezing out the notes, while she pumped the bellows with her feet. And sometimes she joined in the singing, which made us laugh. We heard the Christmas story again, which never lost its magic for us, and I waited for the line, 'to find Mary and Joseph and the Babe lying in a manger,' at which I whispered, 'Bit of a squash,' to make Mum giggle.

Our favourite part was when people returned from communion, the long, self-conscious walk down the aisle. Some smiled and looked silly, a few bore a thunderous expression, and one or two were studiedly nonchalant, and we assessed their outfits for later comparison. I was disappointed with the standard of dress of the holiday cottage owners who lived in smart places like Oxford and London. They turned out in shabby jackets smelling of moth balls, and horror of horrors, some in wellingtons, or gum boots, as they liked to call them. They were all quite thin, with fine-drawn faces, and I decided their dowdiness was something to do with their being clever, as most of them were. The standard was raised at the last minute by a neighbour in her musquash fur jacket, court shoes and red lipstick, which I noticed she wiped on her hand on the way up.

The last reading was, 'In the beginning was the Word,' which the vicar read with grave emphasis, and the whole church fell silent, listening to the age-old words and the beautiful language of the King James Version. Then it was the last hymn, *O Come All Ye Faithful* which everyone sang at the top of their voices, almost cracking the beams above our heads. We had a final prayer from the vicar, concluding with, 'And I wish you all a very Happy Christmas', and he strolled down the aisle smiling and shaking hands. People kissed us and said 'Happy Christmas Mary and Pat' as we moved to the porch, winding our scarves tightly against the sudden blast of cold.

'It's Christmas Day,' I said in wonderment, and linking arms, we picked our way down the stony track home, trying to avoid the potholes. It was a frosty night, the air was clear, the fells loomed darkly in the distance and the sky was crowded with stars.

'Do you think that is The Star,' I asked, pointing to a very bright one overhead.

'Mm. It could be,' replied my mother, not an authority on the planets, 'the stars are very old.'

And as we walked through a farmyard, dogs pushed their noses under the barn door, sheep were bleating in the field, a cow lowed under a tree nearby, and it seemed then that Bethlehem was not so far away.

CHAPTER NINE

A Quarter of Bulls' Eyes

he sun is dipping to the west and catches the glass of the shop window, warming the rough, cream glaze of the handmade pottery on the top shelf, creating prisms of light at the edges of the wine glasses below and turning the replica of a film star's diamond engagement ring into a small, elliptical fire-ball. On the bottom shelf, attached with a drawing pin from behind, stand cards of tiny penknives with pearlised handles, and beside them, campers' knives, fat with implements vital to the life of a small boy. Deer stalkers, snug in their long leather sheaths, dangle temptingly in between, to be used for nothing more alarming than whittling sticks and gutting small trout caught in the river.

It is 5.30pm, just over a year since we moved in. The shop is half an hour past closing time. Mum and I are perched on the window-sill outside, talking about the day, enjoying the warmth of an early August evening. Hikers, hot and weary, clump down from the fell road, and make for the open door of the shop, parking their enormous rucksacks outside. They buy bottles of orange and lemonade drinks, and large bars of chocolate.

'Any cake?' one boy inquires, and after a quick rummage under the counter, my mother produces a Jamaican gingerbread, which, to my amusement, the boy immediately begins to wolf down straight from the packet. Someone spots the ice-cream sign and requests four choc ices.

'I'll get them,' I offer. Having just consumed one myself I know exactly where they are in the fridge. I am one of our shop's best customers.

A tall polite boy pleases my mother by buying a guide book of local walks and an Ordinance Survey map of the Lakes, choosing one made of cloth with a plastic cover. Already it is worth staying open late.

Then we resume our seat by the window and chat to our customers, who tell us they live in Guildford and London, and discuss the subjects they are studying. They sit on the concrete pavement at the front and stretch out their sunburnt legs, thick socks doubled over their boots. Mum teases them and we all laugh as they try to explain how climbing high mountains with half a house on your back can be classed as fun. She remains unconvinced.

The post was collected at 4.20pm. We handed over the canvas bag of parcels, unlocked the letter box from inside the window and lined up all the letters and postcards on a rubber pad on which Mum had scrawled, in biro, messages and various important reminders, like 'pound sausage', 'pay coal man' and 'b day card for Hilda'. The date stamp made a round imprint and sometimes people request a particularly clear one showing the name of our village. I watched enviously, as, with great expertise, my mother fanned out the letters and gave each a quick dab, completing the task in seconds. At ten, I am too young to be allowed to touch anything connected to the post office. My mother is very strict about this.

After six o' clock the village is quiet, and I leap over the counter and lock the door of the shop, top and bottom, with two hefty bolts which have stood the test of time. The black iron bell jangles as I do it. Then we retire to the kitchen at the back of the house overlooking the garden and the fells, and assemble our supper of salad and tinned salmon.

The shop is a small room, rectangular, but tapering off to a point at the far corner; every space is used to keep stock or display goods. We are separated from the customers by an angular semi-circle of three counters, one being a block of oak which my mother waxes occasionally, enhancing the feathering of the golden grain and the patina of a hundred years. At the side of this counter where we stand are tempting stacks of Kendal mint cake, *Observer's Book of British Birds, Birds' Eggs* and *Wild Flowers*, and some small mesh charity stockings into which people can slip their pennies and half-pennies and sometimes a generous sixpence.

Behind us is a show-case with piles of different chocolate bars and boxes of chocolates. Above, like a row of portly soldiers, stand the sweet jars, containing favourites such as chocolate caramels, bulls' eyes and fruit drops, which we weigh out into quarter pound triangular paper bags which never seem quite big enough. In our early days here, the mice gnawed at one corner of a tall stack of enormous bars of Dairy Milk, just a tiny nibble off each one, so Mum sold them off at a special bargain price. Fortunately now we have our ginger tom, all the mice have emigrated. If a child was asked to define his idea of heaven, living in a sweet shop would appear high on the list, and in this first year the three of us, Mum, Benger and I, have all grown a little chubbier. A traveller would say, 'We have a new chocolate bar out, Mrs Nolan. Do you want to sample one?' and our eyes would gleam.

The middle counter is covered with a selection of Dinky Toys of all sizes, the agricultural vehicles being hot favourites. Boys take them to school in their pockets, and on warm summer playtimes on the Howe, they hammer short sticks into the ground to fence off small fields and farms, then with piles of plucked grass they re-enact hay-making (or as we called it, hay-timing) and harvesting; nobody seems to argue or fight at these times, and I like to hear the murmur of their voices, the 'brrm brrm' of a moving tractor, and the smell of grass as they pile it onto a mini wagon.

Above the toys is a glass show-case containing grown-up gifts; at the moment we have a brush and comb set, two cut glass vases, a shaving mirror, and some ornaments with the words 'A Present from Lakeland' painted on them. We also have a large china cart horse and a wooden cart which are very expensive. The vicar has a bet with Mum that we will never sell them, but I think the horse is beautiful and that someone will not be able to resist it. On the top of this show-case twinkle rows of bottles of fizzy drinks which we are constantly replacing.

On the counter facing the door we have our local pottery. Some is just a plain cream, but recently we discovered a pottery near Penrith we really like: everything is either blue or brown, with cream squiggles and dots on it, mugs, jugs, vases, bowls and large salt jars. It is very exciting to see people admiring it, and even better, buying a few pieces. Holiday-makers are always saying, 'We need to buy something for the person minding the cat,' so we always suggest pottery, as at least it is useful.

I am allowed to help in the shop, to fetch and carry, serve and give change if it's a straightforward transaction, like a packet of sweets or half a dozen postcards, as I am good at my tables and mental arithmetic. My mother thinks it will bring me out of my shell as I am quite shy, particularly of strangers, and I think she is right; and it does feel easier with the counter separating us. I love the postcards, all black and white photographs of the valley, and I help to choose ones I think will be popular. My favourite is of Scafell, with the village nestled below, surrounded by fields, dry stone walls and small clumps of trees.

Ever since our house was built it has always been a shop; the large black hooks on the ceiling probably held hams and sides of bacon, but now there are children's fishing nets dangling from them, kites, washing lines and nets of footballs. Mum says we have something for every occasion: birthdays, wet days, outdoor activities, hungry moments, bored children, small accidents, headaches, navigation in the mountains and many more. We might have to ferret around for a while, but we normally come up with something suitable. You could not produce a feast from our shelves, but two starving campers could make a supper of a couple of tins of stewing steak, a packet of rice, garden peas and a large tin of peaches with some evaporated milk, washed down with a mug of tea and a few custard creams. This would be very satisfying, sitting round your camp-fire under the stars.

We do not have a till, but there are four wooden drawers fitted under the counter. One is for cigarettes and matches; two are for post office papers such as fishing and dog licences, postal orders and stamps, with a wooden box for notes and a yellow and blue tin which says 'Cheese Nibbles' on it for the coins. The shop drawer is smaller, with two compartments for coins and notes. We add up on the back of sweet bags and old envelopes, though we have a proper book of bills if people want it more official. We have to keep the post office money separate from ours which is a big headache, and mum has to balance the accounts

every Friday. At night she empties both cash drawers of their notes, and folds them into her handbag which she takes upstairs to bed, in case of burglars while we are asleep.

Once a year the head-postmaster and his assistant pay a surprise visit, which we dread. They have been twice now, suddenly arriving in the shop with briefcases, wearing grey suits and serious faces.

'Can we check the accounts please, Mrs Nolan?' And they retire to the dining-room with the post office stock and all the money to make sure everything is in order. Afterwards they say something like, 'That's fine Mrs Nolan, just a few pence out.' Then Mum gives them an enormous whisky each with a small jug of water, and they become different people, laughing and joking and buying a packet of cigarettes from us, and Mum's face looks pink and relieved. They pop in to say hello to our old lady, and because she is a bit deaf yell a few things like, 'You're looking well,' or 'Beautiful day today,' as they always seems to choose a sunny day to pay us a visit. Then they run out of conversation.

When we took over the place it looked very different. Mrs Martin was old and tired, and the stock had shrunk to a few sweets, indigestion tablets and cigarettes, and we have gradually built it up, though we have only been able to afford to do it gradually. On the first day after we had filled the shelves and were open for business, I ran all the way home from school in my excitement to see how it had gone.

'What was your first sale?' I asked, puffing into the shop the customer side.

'A bottle of Lucozade,' was the reply. It had been rather quiet actually, and I was a bit disappointed, but Mum said it would take time, and now we are much busier, especially during school holidays.

After Mrs Martin broke her hip, she refused to go to hospital, saying they do you in at places like that, so she was unable to walk and became bed-ridden. Sometimes, while we are serving in the shop she calls out loudly, 'Mary, I want the pan!' She means the bedpan and it's quite embarrassing, as we cannot leave a shop full of customers and she continues to shout. Mum goes as soon as she can, but sometimes it is not soon enough. It was hard though, especially in the first few months when we had to carry water from the beck. It will be better when electricity comes to the village, possibly next year, and we can have hot water running from the taps. What a luxury!

One of the best things about a shop is that you have constant company, and meet a large cross-section of society, which I am told will broaden my mind. Most people in the village take the weekly local paper, and if we aren't too busy, my mother sits on a set of steps with a flat top that we keep by the counter and chats with them, and they sometimes discuss their problems.

In summer we have parties of school children, cubs, scouts and brownies. Our rule is only three children at a time in the shop, plus their leader, and we have to keep a sharp eye on wandering little fingers. They all buy a present for their mums, and we have to suggest various possibilities, like vases for wild flowers and a choice of ornaments. They are all mad for penknives, the more dangerous-looking the better, but the teacher normally forbids such purchases. Key rings are very popular, especially the ones with small silver compasses attached; I would quite like one of these for myself.

We also have the regular holiday cottage owners who come for Easter and most of the summer. They are very friendly, but *will* keep inviting me to tea on Saturday afternoons. I stand behind the show-case making a 'No' face at Mum, as I do not know their children very well, and they all go to posh boarding schools, speak French and sometimes get out the Monopoly board, which is a disaster, as I do not know how to pronounce places like Mary-le-bone and other streets I have never even heard of. But Mum looks pleased and says, 'Thank you very much. I'm sure she would love to come,' and I spend the rest of the week grumbling. This comes under the category of 'things that are good for you'. Fortunately the reality is it usually turns out better than I expect and I enjoy it once I get there and find they are not so grand after all.

My favourite time in the shop is definitely Christmas, which was bitterly cold this year. We placed a few decorations around the shop, trailed some silver tinsel over the pottery and gifts, and filled one of the bigger vases with a bunch of holly which was bursting with scarlet berries. I wanted to put candles in the window, but was not allowed to do so until Christmas Eve, as they were very small and would not last long. I arranged them on the shelves in the window between articles on display, keeping them away from anything flammable.

Then, in the afternoon, as the light started to fade, Mum brought the oil lamp into the shop which became shadowy and mysterious, and I took the matches and carefully lit all the candles. The lights from the window made it seem darker outside, and the fell loomed high, a solid grey; the sky above it looked like a sheet of steel. A sudden gust of wind blew a few stray snowflakes against the glass, making a soft ticking noise. But when I turned round I saw that something quite magical had happened; the tiny flickering flames of the candles were reflected in the glass of the show-cases, the jars and bottles and wine glasses lining the shelves; it seemed as if the whole room shimmered with a thousand candles. I called to Mum next door and she came to look.

'Well,' she said, 'isn't that beautiful!'

I thought of all the hard work of the past months, the scrubbing, polishing, painting, unpacking of orders and arranging displays, which had so exhausted my mother, and suddenly, at that moment, it all became worthwhile.

Scafell

CHAPTER TEN

Last Days

bitter wind blew down the valley and froze my cheek as, yet again, I peered out on to the main road, hoping in vain to see a fawn Austin 35 car appear over the hill.

It was mid-February; we were still under the brittle grip of winter, giving temperatures of well below zero every morning. The fells had retained their coating of snow and the edges of the road were mini glaciers, to be avoided. I shivered; a vest, fleecy liberty-bodice, woolly knee socks folded over garters, warm coat, hat and scarf were becoming an inadequate protection against the cold, and my throat felt as if I had swallowed a pack of needles.

I huddled into the stone wall for shelter, and crossed two fingers inside my mittens that she had not forgotten me.

For today, I had been told, was one of the most important days of my life; it was the eleven-plus examination, to be sat in a village ten miles away at 9am, and it was now nearly 8.30am; my mother would be furious, particularly as I was suffering from tonsillitis and a high temperature.

Meanwhile, just as I was trying to decide what to do, I saw the car shoot over the hill and tear down the road towards me. It pulled up with a screech of brakes and the passenger door was flung open.

'Jump in!' our teacher shouted, and I saw the three boys sitting in the back, grinning. Her face was flushed and she had the appearance of someone who had recently been involved in a skirmish with a gorse-bush; wisps of hair escaping from plaits pinned over her head, buttons on the shoulder of her jumper undone, skirt twisted.

'Oh dear, oh dear! I'm afraid I slept in. What time is it now?'

This question was repeated at five minute intervals till we arrived, and each time I consulted my tenth birthday present, Swiss-made, five jewels, tan leather strap, and gave the latest time signal. We seemed to be travelling at great speed along the road to Seascale which consisted of a series of hairpin bends.

''Ey up!' said William from the back, as yet again the boys landed in a giggling heap in the corner of the seat.

We roared into Seascale at two minutes to nine, Swiss time.

'Off you go! I'll park the car and follow you in to explain,' and the four of us hurried into the school where the examination was to take place. We entered a classroom just as the invigilator was being asked by the Chief of the Eleven Plus if he was ready to start.

'No. We're waiting for the last lot.' He looked grumpy. 'Oh, here they are now.'

We scurried to the vacant places, as our teacher appeared at the door.

'So sorry, so sorry, we were rather delayed...' she panted.

'That's all right, Miss Jackson,' the invigilator said in the sort of voice which indicated the contrary. He turned to us. 'All ready?'

The other examinees sat with papers before them, headings filled in, exuding self-righteousness, gazing at the riff-raff who had just burst in. I scrabbled in my pencil case for the rubber and three pencils my mother had sharpened for me the night before, and then immediately the teacher said in a portentous voice:

'Right everybody. Pick up your pencils, and... begin.'

The first part of the exam was called the Intelligence Test, consisting of twenty short questions. Still slightly out of breath I wrote my name, then whizzed through the test, ticking, crossing, circling and underlining. Then hurriedly I filled in the information, and had time to look over again at what

I had written, and began to feel calmer.

'And… pencils down please. Oh, the late-comers can fill in their details at the top.'

Now he tells us, I thought crossly.

The English paper followed, involving some grammar questions and a comprehension; as instructed I studied the text carefully and left no blanks.

We took a fifteen minute break outside, 'for some fresh air' we were told, though I noticed the adults darted back indoors pretty quickly, as a sharp wind from the sea whipped up our anxieties over the next ordeal, the Maths exam. Pupils from other schools stuck together in large groups; we were the smallest school and huddled in our gang of four, discussing our hair-raising journey of the morning.

Maths was my worst subject. The teacher had arrived at our house one evening bearing her college entrance papers from forty years ago, and we had pored over the problems for ages, neither of us having a clue as to the solution.

'I think this is how you do it,' she would say at last, droplets of her saliva decorating the paper like tiny stars, and I would hurriedly agree.

At the end of the exam Miss Jackson was waiting.

'How was it?' she asked us eagerly, worried that our scramble earlier might have affected our performance.

'It was a' reet,' said Edward.

She looked at me.

'Medium,' I replied.

She took us off to a café where we sat in an embarrassed silence, our faces in glasses of lemonade, nibbling biscuits while she tried to extract some information from us, and as I swallowed I realised my sore throat had miraculously disappeared.

If you passed the eleven plus in our valley, you were sent to board at a grammar school in Keswick, 45 miles away. It also served the day children of the town, and lay on the shores of Derwentwater, with the grey flanks of Skiddaw reclining behind. But if I failed, I would attend a small school three miles down the valley till I was fifteen. As there were no funds for further training, I would probably try for work locally, or even help at home. Much rested on the result, but once the excitement had subsided, I tried to put it out of my mind.

With the approach of spring, we became absorbed in our annual hunt for birds' nests; this year a robin built its cup-shaped nest in a creeper in our garden, and each day deposited a perfect little sky blue egg till there were four of them lying on the mossy bed.

My friends and I took our dogs and followed paths up the fells to wherever they led, discovering remote mountain tarns, and as the warmer weather arrived, swam the length and breadth of them, whilst the dogs flopped in the wiry grass and gazed longingly at the huddles of munching sheep.

One morning towards the end of May, we lolled

over our reading books in the school-room while the teacher sat marking our Maths, sipping a cup of tea. Then she looked up suddenly and stared at me.

Now what? I thought.

'Oh, Mary,' she said. I had by now learned to answer to my first name.

'Yes?'

'You've passed.' She seemed breathless and was beaming at me, which was unusual.

I looked at the books and thought for a moment she was referring to the test we had completed that morning, but then I saw she was holding a letter.

'You've got the scholarship.'

'Have I?'

'Heck!' said everybody, and my friend patted me on the back saying, 'Well done!' I felt an enormous smile creeping up, with a feeling of intense relief.

'Would you like to go home and tell your mother?' There was no telephone in the school. 'Take my bicycle,' she said, 'oh, and get me half a dozen two-pence-halfpenny stamps while you're there,' and she handed me a ten shilling note.

I stepped outside and stood for a moment, trying to absorb the news. It was what my mother sometimes called a halcyon day, completely still, without a breath of wind; of soft hazy sunshine, the sort of day something quite magical could happen. And it had.

I peddled furiously up the road on the teacher's old bike, basket at the front, rattle coming from the back mud-guard, and the smile on my face remained. I smiled at Bill in his horse and cart.

'How do Bill. I've passed!' But I don't think he got the message.

I smiled at the bluebells by the roadside, at birds along the telephone wires and at the invisible cuckoo calling to me from a nearby wood.

When I arrived in the village I found our tiny shop was full of Irishmen who were laying electricity cables in the street. They were chatting to Mum and playing with Muffin the Mule on the counter, trying to get the magnetic carrot into its mouth. I joined the queue, but was too impatient to wait.

'Mum!' I called.

She looked up and smiled.

'Hello Pat. What are you doing here at this time of day?'

'Mum, I've passed!'

I will never forget the expression of pure joy on her face.

'What's she passed?' all the men wanted to know, and for a few minutes I basked in their congratulations and praise. Then I bought the teacher's stamps, went to hug my dog and returned to school, making large zigzags on the road to delay my journey back.

That evening I was allowed to celebrate in whatever way I chose; so after the shop closed at five, we set off with a picnic up a fell on the sunny side of the valley, accompanied by my best friend

and her sister. We sat nibbling salmon sandwiches
and chocolate biscuits, talking of serious things. My
mother warned me it would be a big change in my
life; of course she would miss me, but that it was a
tremendous opportunity which shouldn't be wasted.

'What are you looking forward to most?'
everyone asked.

'Midnight feasts,' I would reply immediately. I
was immersed in Enid Blyton's *Mallory Towers* books,
and could not wait to begin my big adventure.

There followed weeks of feverish preparation, the
procuring of uniform, both new and second-hand, the
stitching of endless name-tapes. Excitement mounted.

But a fortnight before the beginning of term,
whilst I was performing a daring tight-rope walk
across an iron fence in the vicarage garden, I toppled
and fell, catching my wrist on the top rung. It was
pronounced broken, and was encased in a plaster cast.
To my mother's great annoyance, all the cream viyella
blouses had to be slit to the elbow, to be stitched up
again when the cast was removed.

The moment finally arrived; a soft day in early
September with a morning mist and a nip in the air. I
proudly put on the bottle green tunic, blouse, stripy tie,
green cardigan and hefty brogues. My plaits had been
cruelly chopped to a short bob, giving me a change
of identity. Mum appeared with her box camera and
took my photo on the Mill Bridge, a lanky girl with
a reluctant smile. A neighbour who was giving me a

lift arrived in his old Jowett with his daughter who
attended the same school. I cuddled the dog and kissed
Mum goodbye. We were all smiles.

'Be a good girl. Work hard!'

''Course I will!'

Loading bracken on the hill above Boot

As we chugged off I turned to wave goodbye, to the blue shadowed fell and the green pool where we had swum, to Benger racing after the car, silky ears flapping and mouth open as if he were laughing; to the village, and to Mum, standing on the step, hand in the air, still smiling.

When we reached the corner I burst into tears.

left the valley that day, returning only for holidays. But I discovered in the years to come that I have carried it inside me – that place and that time – ever since.

My mother died on 4th September 2002, two days before her eighty-eighth birthday. We held her funeral in the small church by the river, a mile away from the road, and buried her in the churchyard where generations of my family lay. The weather had been stormy, but on this day it was very still, with a pale sunlight filtering through.

It was a good turn-out, she would have said. We all filed out of church to the graveside as the strains of Fauré's *In Paradisum* floated after us. I dropped two scented roses from her garden onto the coffin. They slipped down the side but the vicar stooped and placed them on the lid.

Beneath Scafell's milky blue summit and a scattering of wispy clouds, I grieved at her passing, and for memories of a world – the world into which I was born and which is now gone for ever.

GRIP   PAT

N Cumbrian households cooking played an important part in daily lives; meals were required to be tasty and sustaining with ingredients that were readily available. Many recipes have been passed down through families for generations, each bearing small changes and additions, subtly differentiating them from the same dish served up next door.

These are some of our favourites.

MOTHER'S RECIPE FOR TATIE-POT

A lovely warming dish served in the pubs after a long day's hunting on the fells.

Serves 6

INGREDIENTS
675g neck/breast/loin of Herdwick lamb, cubed
1 tbs light oil
1 tbs plain flour
100g black pudding, skinned and sliced
1 large onion, peeled and sliced
3 medium carrots, peeled and chopped
Salt and freshly ground pepper
1 pint hot water or beef stock
2 bay leaves
bunch of fresh thyme
450g potatoes, thinly sliced on the diagonal
25g butter

METHOD

1) Preheat oven to 200°C/400°F

2) Heat oil in a pan, brown the meat and sprinkle over flour. Transfer to an oven-proof roasting dish.

3) Add the black pudding, carrots, onions, bay leaf and thyme and season well.

4) Arrange the potato slices on top, like slates on a roof.

5) Add water or stock to cover meat and vegetables but not potatoes.

6) Dot the potatoes with butter, cover and place in the oven for about 90 mins. Add more water during cooking if dish becomes dry.

7) Remove lid or foil and cook for a further 30 mins or until brown on top.

We always served it with pickled red cabbage.

CUMBERLAND RUM NICKY

A traditional dish to warm the cockles when autumn days are drawing in or to stave off the raw winter weather! And perfect on return from the show, tired and ravenous! As with Rum Butter it probably originated in the late 1700s when trade with the Caribbean brought rum, molasses and spices into the port of Whitehaven. 'Nicky' might refer to the nicks made in the pastry topping to aid cooking, or possibly some ingredients had to be nicked, or – this was my favourite explanation – it was he preferred dish of Old Nick himself!

You can vary the fruit used, currants, apple rather than apricots, but keep the ginger and the rum.

Serves 6+

INGREDIENTS

225g medjool dates, pitted and chopped
110g dried apricots, chopped
50g crystallised ginger, finely chopped, without the juice
glass of rum (approx. 50ml)
40g of dark brown sugar
50g butter, cut into small cubes
pinch of nutmeg
20cm flan tin
450g short crust pastry

METHOD

1) Mix together all the ingredients minus the butter and mash a little with a fork so that it resembles mincemeat. Leave for half an hour or so to allow the flavours to mingle.

2) Roll out the pastry thinly. You can either a) line small cake tins, fill with fruit and place over them a pastry topping, as with mince pies, or b) divide the pastry in two parts, two-thirds and a third, placing the

larger piece on the plate, allowing it to overlap a little.

3) Pour in the fruit mixture, smooth out and dot with the butter.

4) If you are feeling artistic you can cut the second sheet of pastry into strips and make a lattice pattern over the fruit, weaving in the strips neatly till they reach the edge. Nip the edges together with finger and thumb, using the overlap part and a brush of water to help it stick. Otherwise just place the second piece on top and attach round the edge. Do not forget the nicks!

5) Brush the top with beaten white of egg and place in a preheated oven of 180°C/350°F for 15 mins, then lower heat to 160°C/325°F for a further 15-20 mins. Check that the edges do not catch.

Serve warm or cold with cream or ice-cream.

PACE EGGS

In the days before Easter, we began to turn our minds to the exciting business of making Pace eggs (thought to be a derivation of the word Pâcques, French for Easter). There is a multitude of methods and preferences concerning the dying of eggs, but in our valley the basic ingredient for this process was always a pile of onion skins, which, if you were organised, you began to save a week or two in advance.

To make these traditional little works of art you will need:

a collection of large eggs at room temperature

onion skins, brown or red, a mixture of the two is effective

several handfuls of gorse flowers, when available

a few primrose flowers (optional)

torn petals of daffodils or other yellow flowers (optional)

newspaper, white string or kitchen foil a large old pan

THE PROCESS:

We always used newspaper, approximately the size of one tabloid sheet per egg, tied up in a parcel with string, but a piece of kitchen foil 20x20cm also works well and is simpler.

1) Form a small pile of crumpled onions skin on the sheet of paper or foil, run the egg under the tap and lay it on its aromatic bed.

2) Gently place a primrose flower(s) of choice on the shell,

smoothing down the petals. My mother always liked to wind a daffodil leaf round the middle of the egg to make a ribbon effect. Scatter some of your petal collection over the egg and fold firmly into a parcel, covering the surface of the shell with onion skins and petals.

3) Place your parcels in a pan of warm water and bring to the boil. Turn down the heat to avoid cracking and allow to bubble gently for 10-15 minutes. We often left them for longer.

4) Remove from the heat and allow to cool.

5) Carefully lift each parcel from the pan, allowing the liquid to drain, and place on a large plate. Now for the exciting moment when your miraculous little gems are revealed. Undo each parcel and slowly extract the egg, just like removing a conker from its prickly husk. Wipe clean and rub a small dab of butter over the shell to give a shine and accentuate the rich colours.

On Easter Sunday or Monday we rolled the eggs down a hill, the winner being the one with the least number of cracks. This is a symbol of the stone being rolled away from Jesus's tomb.

It was the custom to give an egg to each of your visitors over the Easter period. Some could not bear to eat them but kept them till they became very light, eventually turning to dust inside!

Finally the eggs are eaten with hot cross buns, toasted or heated in the oven, with plenty of butter, salt and pepper. Delicious!

SCRUMPTIOUS LEMON PUDDING

One of our favourite puddings which cheered us up when we needed it most.

Serves 2-3

INGREDIENTS

1 large tbs butter
¾ cup sugar
1½ cups of milk
2 lemons
2 eggs
2 tbs self-raising flour

METHOD
1) Cream softened butter and sugar and add flour. Mix well.
2) Stir in juice and rind of both lemons.
3) Beat egg yolks and milk and add to the mixture.
4) Add egg whites, beaten stiffly.
5) Mix gently, transfer into a greased dish and place in a container of shallow water.
6) Bake in a moderate oven until golden brown – approximately ¾ hour.
7) Serve with cream!

MARY'S CUMBERLAND RUM BUTTER
As sold in the Post Office for many years

This delicacy is traditionally served at christenings and at Christmas. A large rum butter bowl is still a treasured part of many a Cumbrian family's heritage. Rum was imported from the Caribbean into several west Cumbrian harbours, Whitehaven in particular being a leading port for the rum trade. As the story goes, butter is for the richness of life, sugar for the sweetness and rum for the spirit!

There are many variations of the recipe, but this was ours.

INGREDIENTS

225g butter
225g of soft brown sugar, plus one extra handful
a third of a nutmeg, freshly grated
1 generous glass of rum (or two) to taste

METHOD
1) Mix sugar and grate nutmeg.
2) Melt the butter and stir into the sugar mixture.
3) Add the rum and stir vigorously with a wooden spoon till smooth.
4) A short spin with a whisk adds lightness to the dish.
5) Taste and add more rum if necessary, mixing thoroughly.

Rum butter is delicious served on oat cakes, cream crackers, scones and with Christmas pudding. It also makes a tasty addition to ice-cream.

SNOW PANCAKES

I always loved the idea of this recipe and nagged my mother to make it as soon as the first snowflake hit the window. But the rule was it has to be the right kind of snow (not the wet, heavy sort), so I had to be patient. I think the pleasure of this dish was in the making of it!

INGREDIENTS (for one pancake)

1 heaped tbs plain flour
3 tbs milk
Pinch of salt
1 tbs of fine powdery snow

METHOD

1) Mix flour and milk to a stiff batter.
2) Add the snow and stir in gently.
3) Fry in butter or oil, whichever you prefer.
4) Serve with jam or fruit.

THE LAST SUPPER

On my last day at home before leaving for boarding school my mother asked me, 'What would you like for supper tonight? You can choose anything, within reason.'

It was rather like the prisoner's last request before execution but I knew the answer without having to think about it.

'Cumberland sausage,' I replied. I don't know why we always called it Cumberland sausage when we already lived there, but it was probably to differentiate between the thick meaty variety and those small pink sausages from a packet that looked like dead fingers.

The sausage (half a pound) had to be pricked and baked in the oven rather than fried. We preferred it brown all over with no pale stripes at the sides, and liked it when bits oozed out of each end and turned lovely and crispy.

MASHED POTATO was beaten with salt and pepper, a knob of butter and a slosh of milk which was not graded at that time so you had two or three inches of cream on the top.

APPLE SAUCE – always. We peeled and chopped a Bramley apple, added a little sugar and water and simmered it in a pan till it was soft. Then it was beaten with a fork and put to one side.

The VEGETABLES were carrots and peas, chosen for their sweet clean flavour which complemented the creaminess of the potato, the tartness of the apple sauce and the spicy chunkiness of the sausage. Vegetables

140

like mange-touts, sugar snap peas or asparagus tips were not an option then, but I would still have made the same choice.

And NO GRAVY – ever. Too sloppy and spoiled the flavours.

Dessert was a slice of ice-cream from the shop fridge, probably Raspberry Ripple or maybe Viennese Coffee as I thought that was rather exotic.

It all turned out perfectly. As we savoured our feast, sitting low at the kitchen table (low as we had had to cut several inches off each leg to angle it through the door), we watched the light softening over the fells, turning Harter fell pink and the garden a pale greeny blue. After a wet August it seemed unfair that the weather should suddenly turn warm and sunny just at the moment I had to leave it all behind.

Patricia on her beloved Fells with a young neighbour

Acknowledgements

My friends for their loyal support.
Fellow writers for their honest opinions.
Margot Stedman, godmother to the book, with special gratitude, without whose encouragement and insistence that the stories had a voice, they would still be sitting on my computer.
The people of the valley who share my memories.
My publishers, Karen McCall and Merlin Unwin, for their enthusiasm and creativity in miraculously transforming my childhood memories into a beautiful book.

Photo credits

The Cumbria Image Bank: pp43, 61
Geoff Todd: p53
Joseph Hardman Collection: p63
Bob Kennard, from *Much Ado About Mutton*: p84
Helen Shaw, from *The Pennines*: p95
Cumberland & Westmorland Antiquarian & Archaeological Society: p127
Shutterstock: pp6, 18, 28, 75, 61, 89, 96, 113, 118, 128
All other photographs: author's private collection

Also published by Merlin Unwin Books

Much Ado about Mutton Bob Kennard

Recollections of a Moorland Lad Richard Robinson

The Pennines - England's Backbone Helen Shaw

Wildlife of the Pennine Hills Doug Kennedy

The Yellow Earl Douglas Sutherland

Myddle – The Life & Times of a Shropshire Farmworker's Daughter 1911-1928 Helen Ebrey

The Flood – Surviving the Deluge Michael Brown

My Animals and Other Family – A Rural Childhood 1937-1956 Phyllida Barstow

A Job for all Seasons – My Small Country Living Phyllida Barstow

Beneath Safer Skies – A Child Evacuee in Shropshire Anthea Toft

The WI Country Woman's Year 1960

Pull the Other One – Britain's Favourite Dairy Farmer Roger Evans

The Way of a Countryman Ian Niall

The Countryman's Creel Conor Farrington

Available from all good bookshops
Full details: **www.merlinunwin.co.uk**

143